Audio Access Included

BASSIST'S GUIDE
SCALES OVER CHORDS
The Foundation of Effective Bass Lines

by Chad Johnson

To access audio visit:
www.halleonard.com/mylibrary
Enter Code
5460-6308-6052-9132

ISBN 978-1-4950-4820-3

HAL•LEONARD®
CORPORATION
7777 W. BLUEMOUND RD. P.O. BOX 13819 MILWAUKEE, WI 53213

In Australia Contact:
Hal Leonard Australia Pty. Ltd.
4 Lentara Court
Cheltenham, Victoria, 3192 Australia
Email: ausadmin@halleonard.com.au

Visit Hal Leonard Online at
www.halleonard.com

CONTENTS

INTRODUCTION

Welcome to *Bassist's Guide to Scales Over Chords*. This book is aimed at the late-beginner or intermediate bassist who's looking to increase his or her familiarity with harmony as it relates to the bass, thereby expanding the depth and scope of his or her playing. The title mentions scales and *chords*, which may seem a little odd, since we don't often play chords on the bass. However, with a firm grasp of music theory, creating effective, melodic bass lines becomes much easier, and that's where this book comes in. Specifically, this book will help players who:

- Know some scales but don't know what to do with them.
- Don't understand how chord progressions work.
- Don't understand the connection between scales and chords.
- Have learned a bunch of bass lines or licks but don't know where to apply them or how to use them in different keys.
- Are stuck in a root-notes rut.
- Don't know the notes on the entire fretboard.

If any or all of the above apply, you'll no doubt improve by leaps and bounds by working through the material in this book. However, this is not a beginner's book with regard to bass technique or music reading; it's assumed that you've already developed some technical ability in both hands and can read the notes on a bass clef (you don't have to be a proficient reader, though, as tab is included for most of the examples, as well). None of the examples in this book are particularly difficult to play, but they're certainly beyond the level of a complete beginner. If you did happen to purchase the book as a complete beginner, don't fret. I'd suggest putting it aside for a bit and developing a bit of bass technique first by way of a beginner method or a private instructor. When you feel ready to tackle most of the examples in Chapter 3, you're ready for this book.

Many self-taught bassists fill their roles in local bands by mostly "duping" what the guitarist is doing—playing root notes. Some learn other strategies for connecting these root notes, thereby adding a bit more motion to their lines. Still, many players end their musical exploration there, drawing on their limited well of knowledge for the rest of their musical lives. Granted, some players have managed to mine these resources with great success and forge successful careers by doing so. The majority, however, aren't as fortunate and end up feeling musically spent or burned out, with no direction.

Learning the bass lines of the masters is certainly a great way to find inspiration and expand your fretboard knowledge, but unless you're able to glean the inner workings behind these lines, your ability to apply or modify them will be severely limited. It's kind of like knowing one specific situation in which you can use a word but not really knowing what the word *truly* means because you've never looked it up in the dictionary.

In this book, you'll learn to make the critical connection between notes, scales, and chords (harmony). This will empower you in more ways than one. You'll be able to imitate what you hear more easily, which will aid in your ability to communicate with other musicians and will help in improvisatory situations. You'll be able to play what you hear in your head more easily, which will help avoid lots of "hunting and pecking" on the fretboard when looking for a specific note. You'll be armed with a myriad of strategies when composing bass lines, enabling you to try several different angles to see what sounds best. And, perhaps most important of all, your confidence as a player will grow exponentially, which has numerous benefits of its own across the board.

So clear your head, grab your bass, and let us commune with the largest of wavelengths.

ABOUT THE AUDIO

When making the connection between scales and chords, it's helpful to hear one against the other. Therefore, most of the audio examples in this book contain full backing with drums and guitars and/or keys. The examples with audio will be marked throughout with the 🔊 symbol. Not only will you get some good metronome practice (as all examples are played to a click), but you'll also be able to hear the connection between harmony and scale.

It's also fun to jam with a friend when working on this stuff. If you know a guitarist or keyboardist, try playing some of the examples with them, as live musical interaction is always a valuable exercise. Try having them play rhythm above you or leads, as well. You may find yourself modifying your lines in response to what they're doing. And, if you're inclined, try playing a solo of your own.

All examples recorded, mixed, and mastered by Chad Johnson at Magnetized World Studio in Denton, Texas. All instruments/programming performed by Chad Johnson.

ABOUT THE AUTHOR

Chad Johnson is a freelance author, editor, and musician. For Hal Leonard Corporation, he's authored over 70 instructional books covering a variety of instruments and topics, including *Teach Yourself to Play Bass Guitar*, *Bass Fretboard Workbook*, *All About Bass*, *How to Record at Home on a Budget*, *Guitarist's Guide to Scales over Chords*, and *Ukulele Aerobics*, to name but a few. He's a featured instructor on the DVD *200 Country Guitar Licks* (also published by Hal Leonard) and has toured and performed throughout the East Coast in various bands, sharing the stage with members of Lynyrd Skynyrd, the Allman Brothers Band, and others. He works as a session instrumentalist, composer/songwriter, and recording engineer when not authoring or editing, and his latest band, Sun City, recently released their self-titled debut album, which can be purchased at *www.suncitymusic.bandcamp.com*. Chad currently resides in Denton, Texas (North Dallas) with his wife and two children, and keeps busy with an active freelance career. If you have any questions or concerns, feel free to contact him at *chadjohnsonguitar@gmail.com*.

ACKNOWLEDGMENTS

I'd like to thank all the folks at Hal Leonard Corporation for their hard work and expertise. It's always a pleasure collaborating with them in every way. Special thanks go to my editor, Kurt Plahna, for his invaluable contributions to the book.

I'd like to dedicate this book to my wife, Alli, and our children, Lennon and Leherie.
A prouder husband and daddy you won't find anywhere.

CHAPTER 1: BASIC SCALE REVIEW

If you purchased this book before learning any scales, then you're in good hands. After reading this chapter, you'll be well-equipped to make the most out of everything you learn from the beginning. If you, like most, already know several scales and bought this book to help make sense of them, consider this chapter a refresher course. It's a vital one, though, so don't skip it! Many concepts mentioned here lay the groundwork for the chapters to come.

MAJOR SCALE

Let's put first things first: The major scale is by far the most important scale you'll ever learn. In fact, the entire system of Western harmony is based on its intervallic structure. In Chapter 2, we'll look more closely at some theory as it relates to the scale, but for now, let's talk a bit about its structure.

Intervals

An *interval* describes the musical distance between two notes. In terms of scales, intervals are usually measured in *half steps* (one fret on the same string of the bass) and *whole steps* (two frets on the same string). A major scale has seven different notes (the "eighth" note is simply a repetition of the first note, but in another octave), and each note is assigned a number: 1, 2, 3, etc. The *intervallic formula* for any major scale is always the same:

Whole step–**W**hole step–**H**alf step–**W**hole step–**W**hole step–**W**hole step–**H**alf step

So, from the first note (1) to the second note (2), the distance is one whole step, or two frets. The distance from 2 to 3 is also one whole step, or two frets. The distance from 3 to 4 is a *half* step, or one fret, and so on. This is demonstrated with the C major scale below:

C Major Scale

TRACK 1

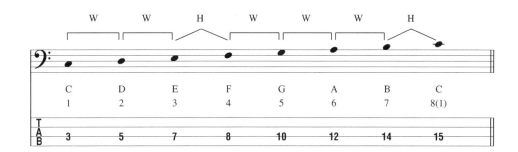

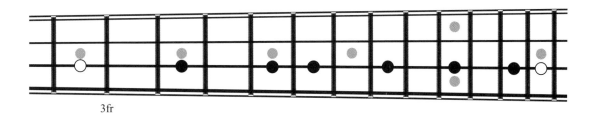

3fr

Note: In this book, the tonic will be represented in the scale diagrams with an open (white) circle.

The Tonic

The first degree (1) of a scale is called the *tonic*; you can think of it as home base. This note feels resolved when you play it. You'll sometimes hear this term used interchangeably with "root." Also, you may notice that, sometimes in this book, the tonic appears at the top of a scale, in a new octave, where it can be labeled as "8," and sometimes it does not. Don't be confused by this. Remember that a major scale has seven *different* notes. The "eighth" note, if it does appear, is just the same as the first, only an octave higher. It's sometimes helpful to see this eighth note—as when using our intervallic formula (W–W–H–W–W–W–H), for example—so you can see that the interval from the 7th to the tonic is a half step.

It's obviously not very practical to play scales all along one string like this, but it's a great way in the beginning to see the whole step/half step intervallic formula at work. In order to make this a more practical scale shape, we can move notes 3, 4, and 5 to the second string, and notes 6, 7, and 8 to the first, like this:

C Major Scale

TRACK 2

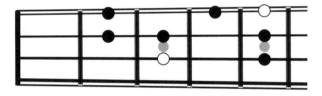

What's great about the bass is that it's so easy to transpose material. In order to make this a D major scale, for instance, all we need to do is move the shape up the neck so that the tonic note is D. This means moving everything up two frets.

D Major Scale

TRACK 3

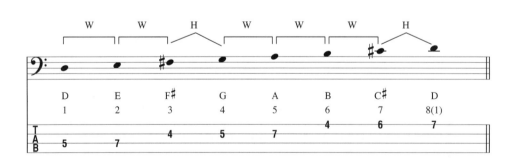

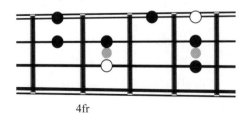

4fr

Notice that we've added some *accidentals* (sharps or flats) to this scale. In order to preserve our formula, W–W–H–W–W–W–H, we had to add two sharps: F♯ and C♯. This wasn't necessary in the key of C, because the interval from E to F and from B to C is naturally a half step. A piano keyboard is especially useful in this regard, where the C major scale lays out on nothing but white keys.

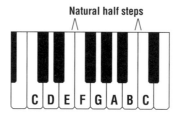

C major is the only major scale that doesn't require any sharps or flats; every other major scale will require at least one sharp or flat (but never both). We'll look more at the theory behind this in Chapter 2.

Major Scale Shapes

So now that we know how it's built, let's look at some C major scale shapes on the bass. Again, the tonics in all the diagrams are indicated with an open circle—in this case, all the C notes. The shapes may contain some notes above or below the tonic if they're within the fretboard position. (On the audio, all examples begin ascending with the tonic note; notes below the tonic, if any, will be included at the end of the descent through the shape.)

Our first C major scale shape begins with the second finger and is based in second position. This is the one we saw earlier. The low tonic is on string 3.

C Major Scale – Shape 1

TRACK 4

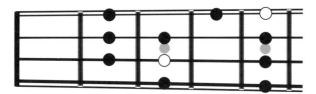

And here's our second shape, which is similar to Shape 1, but it's moved down a string set. Consequently, we don't have as many notes available below the tonic, but we have more above it.

C Major Scale – Shape 2

TRACK 5

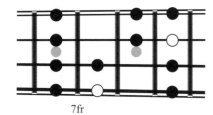

7fr

Here's one that begins with the pinky on string 4. It's based in fifth and fourth position.

C Major Scale – Shape 3

TRACK 6

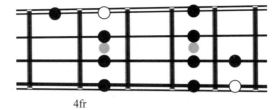

4fr

If these shapes are new to you at all, practice them with a metronome until you can play through them cleanly at a moderate tempo. Sixteenth notes played at approximately 72 beats per minute (bpm) is adequate for now.

MAJOR PENTATONIC SCALE

The major pentatonic scale is simply a five-note version ("penta" means "five") of the seven-note major scale. We simply remove the fourth and seventh notes of the major scale, which leaves the notes 1–2–3–5–6. In the C major scale, this means we eliminate F (4th) and B (7th), leaving the notes C–D–E–G–A.

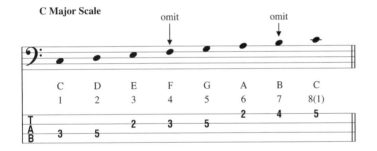

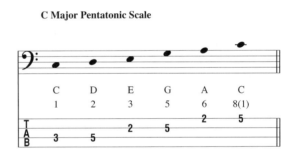

Major Pentatonic Scale Shapes

Now let's take a look at a few C major pentatonic scale shapes that will prove useful. Notice that these shapes are very similar to the major scale shapes you just learned; we've just eliminated two notes. Be sure that you can play these cleanly at a moderate tempo before looking too far ahead in the book. The first shape begins with the second finger on the low tonic (string 3) and is based in second position.

C Major Pentatonic Scale – Shape 1

TRACK 7

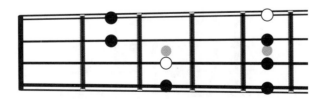

The second shape begins with the second finger on string 4 and is based in seventh position.

C Major Pentatonic Scale – Shape 2

TRACK 8

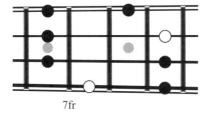

7fr

And here are two more shapes that contain some position shifts—a very common move when dealing with pentatonic scales, since many finger-friendly box positions are created. Both of these begin with the first finger.

C Major Pentatonic Scale – Shape 3

TRACK 9

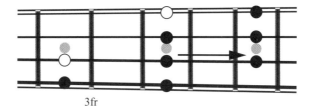

3fr

C Major Pentatonic Scale – Shape 4

TRACK 10

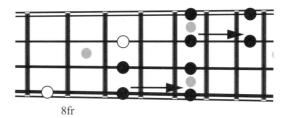

8fr

MINOR SCALE

The minor scale is another seven-note scale, but it has an intervallic formula that is different from the major scale. Whereas the major scale sounds happy or bright, the minor scale sounds sad or dark. There are two ways that you can think about the construction of the minor scale. First, you can approach it from its intervallic formula:

Whole step–**H**alf step–**W**hole step–**W**hole step–**H**alf step–**W**hole step–**W**hole step

We can also build it by altering the scale degrees of the major scale. This is another common way to look at scales. We treat the major scale as the standard, with its degrees numbered 1–7, and then we alter those degrees (raise or lower them by a half step) to create other scales.

To build a minor scale, we need to lower (flat) by a half step the third, sixth, and seventh tones of the major scale. So its scale degrees would be numbered—i.e., it's *numeric formula* is—1–2–♭3–4–5–♭6–♭7. This is demonstrated with the C minor scale below. Compare this to the one-string C major scale on page 7 to see the different intervallic structure.

C Minor Scale

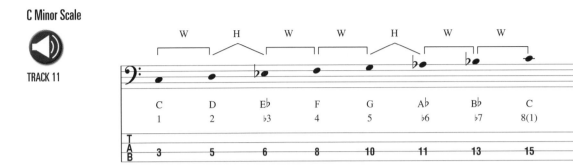

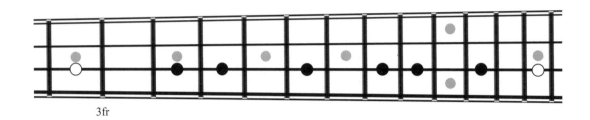

Notice that we've added three flats to spell this scale: E♭, A♭, and B♭. A C minor scale is said to be the *parallel minor* of C major because they share the same tonic: C. We'll talk more about this concept later.

C Minor Scale Shapes

Here are two different C minor scale shapes to learn. The first shape is in third position, beginning with your index finger on the low tonic of string 3.

C Minor Scale – Shape 1

TRACK 12

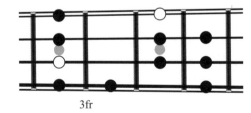

This second shape is similar to the first, only we've shifted it down a string set. It begins with the first finger and is based mostly around eighth position.

C Minor Scale – Shape 2

TRACK 13

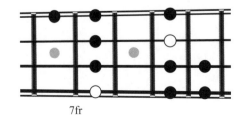

MINOR PENTATONIC SCALE

Just like the major scale and its companion major pentatonic, the minor scale has a five-note version called the *minor pentatonic scale*. To build it, we again eliminate two notes from the minor scale: the 2nd and ♭6th. So the minor pentatonic scale degrees are numbered 1–♭3–4–5–♭7. In the C minor scale, this means we eliminate D (2nd) and A♭ (♭6th), leaving the notes C–E♭–F–G–B♭.

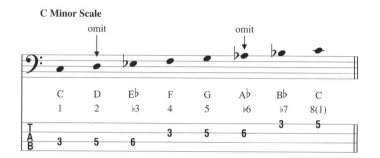

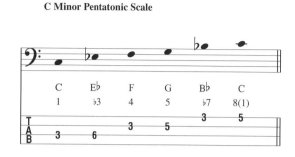

Minor Pentatonic Scale Shapes

Now let's look at some minor pentatonic scale shapes. The first is in third position and begins with the index finger on the low tonic of string 3.

C Minor Pentatonic Scale – Shape 1

TRACK 14

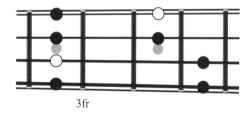

3fr

The second shape begins with the first finger, as well, and is found in eighth position.

C Minor Pentatonic Scale – Shape 2

TRACK 15

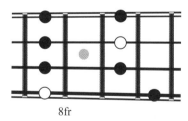

8fr

And here's one more for good measure. This one is found in sixth and fifth position and places the tonic on string 4, which is played with your pinky.

C Minor Pentatonic Scale – Shape 3

TRACK 16

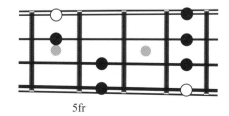

5fr

TRANSPOSING THE SHAPES

Again, one of the great things about the bass is its ease in transposition. Since they contain no open strings, all of the shapes we learned here are moveable and can be easily transposed to other keys (besides C) simply by moving them up or down the neck. How is this done? It's easy! All you need to know are the names of the notes along the fourth and third strings. And here they are:

Notes on the Fourth and Third Strings

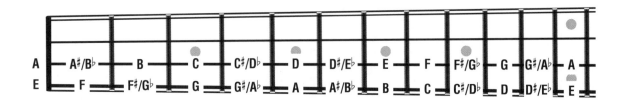

After the 12th fret, the order starts all over again. So, on string 4, fret 13 is F, fret 14 is F#/G♭, and so on. So, let's say you want to play Shape 2 of the minor pentatonic scale in the key of A minor. Simply slide the shape down so that the tonic note on the fourth string is on the note A, and you have an A minor pentatonic scale. Since A is on the fifth fret of the fourth string, your A minor pentatonic shape would look like this:

A Minor Pentatonic Scale – Shape 2

TRACK 17

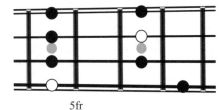

5fr

Or let's say you want to play the E major scale using Shape 1. Find E on string 3 and slide the shape until the tonic note matches that location. Since E is on fret 7 of the third string, your E major scale shape would look like this:

E Major Scale – Shape 1

TRACK 18

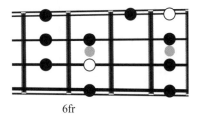

6fr

See if you can find the following scale shapes. Answers are at the bottom of the next page (no peeking!).

- B Minor Scale – Shape 1
- D Major Pentatonic Scale – Shape 2
- B♭ Major Pentatonic Scale – Shape 4
- G Minor Pentatonic Scale – Shape 2

OK, so now we've learned how to construct and play four of the most common scales in all of music: the major scale, the major pentatonic, the minor scale, and the minor pentatonic. Believe it or not, this is where a good many players stop learning. They learn a few phrases from these scales and never bother to learn why they sound the way they do—or, more importantly, why they seem to work sometimes and not others.

Afraid to Step out of the Comfort Zone

We've all seen those players who play literally the *same exact thing* every time they play a song. This could, of course, be because the bass line was handed down by the gods and is the picture of perfection. More often, though, it's because the player is limited in his knowledge and dare not step out of his comfort zone lest he hit a sour note. When the fretboard looks like a dark forest of winding branches that crisscross in every direction, it makes sense that one would be afraid to step off the beaten path. This situation is not uncommon; it's what happens to many players who, for whatever reason, decide not to progress by learning more than just a few shapes on the fretboard.

It doesn't have to be that way, though. To many players, the fretboard looks like a well-organized file cabinet, with each document clearly marked for quick and easy accessibility. You're about to take the first step in breaking past this barrier that holds so many players back. Read on!

WHAT YOU LEARNED:

- Intervallic construction of the major and minor scales.
- Construction of the major and minor pentatonic scales.
- Several fingering patterns for major and major pentatonic scales.
- Several fingering patterns for minor and minor pentatonic scales.
- How to transpose the fingering patterns to any other tonic.

Answer Key

G Minor Pentatonic Scale – Shape 2

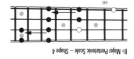

B♭ Major Pentatonic Scale – Shape 4

D Major Pentatonic Scale – Shape 2

B Minor Scale – Shape 1

CHAPTER 2: DIATONIC HARMONY PRIMER

Before we start laying it down, we need to learn some fundamentals that will pay off in a big way down the line. The knowledge presented in this chapter will open the doors to a lifetime of learning and improvement on the bass. These are the important first steps.

So, what exactly does the term "diatonic harmony" mean? The word "diatonic" stems from a Greek word that roughly means "progressing through tones." For our purposes, it basically means "in key" or "belonging to one key." For example, we would say that the notes of the C major scale (C–D–E–F–G–A–B) are diatonic to the key of C major. Any other notes—E♭ or B♭, for example—are not diatonic (or non-diatonic) to the key of C major. Make sense?

MORE ON INTERVALS

A musical interval has two components: *quantity and quality*. The quantity is expressed numerically; for example, we say that C and E are a 3rd apart. This is because there are three note names involved in the distance between them, and we confirm this by counting forward through the musical alphabet: **C** (1)–D (2)–**E** (3). By the same token, C and G would be a 5th apart: **C** (1)–D (2)–E (3)–F (4)–**G** (5). The notes D and E would be a 2nd apart: **D** (1)–**E** (2). What about from G to C? Remember that the musical alphabet only goes from A to G; after G, we start over at A. Therefore, from G to C would be a 4th: **G** (1)–A (2)–B (3)–**C** (4).

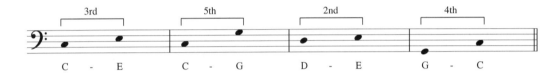

That's really all there is to the quantity. It's pretty simple. The *quality* is where most of the action lies. There are seven different notes in a diatonic major scale (or minor scale), but there are 12 total notes in an octave when you include the non-diatonic tones, as well. (In other words, if you counted every key on a piano—black and white—between one note and the same note an octave higher, you'd get 12.) And this is where the quality comes in.

There are five types of qualities used to describe intervals: *major, minor, augmented, diminished,* and *perfect.* The chart below shows the intervals for all 12 notes of the octave measured against a C root note. I know it may look intimidating right now, but don't fret. It will all make sense soon enough.

Notes	# of half steps	Interval Name	Abbreviation
C to C	0	Unison	P1
C to D♭	1	Minor 2nd	m2
C to D	2	Major 2nd	M2
C to E♭	3	Minor 3rd	m3
C to E	4	Major 3rd	M3
C to F	5	Perfect 4th	P4
C to F♯ C to G♭	6	Augmented 4th Diminished 5th	A4 d5
C to G	7	Perfect 5th	P5
C to A♭	8	Minor 6th	m6
C to A	9	Major 6th	M6
C to B♭	10	Minor 7th	m7
C to B	11	Major 7th	M7
C to C	12	Octave	P8

From this chart, we can deduce a lot about interval qualities. Here are some of the axioms on display:

1. **A minor interval is one half step *smaller* than a major interval.**

   C to E (4 half steps) = major 3rd

   C to E♭ (3 half steps) = minor 3rd

2. **An augmented interval is one half step *larger* than a perfect interval.**

   C to F (5 half steps) = perfect 4th

   C to F♯ (6 half steps) = augmented 4th

3. **A diminished interval is one half step *smaller* than a perfect interval.**

   C to G (7 half steps) = perfect 5th

   C to G♭ (6 half steps) = diminished 5th

4. **The terms "major" and "minor" do not apply to 4ths and 5ths.**

   We use "perfect," "augmented," or "diminished" to describe them.

5. **The term "perfect" does not apply to 2nds, 3rds, 6ths, or 7ths.**

   We use "major" or "minor" to describe them, although "diminished" and "augmented" are occasionally used, as well. We can, at times, have augmented 2nds and 6ths, which are one half step larger than major 2nds and 6ths, respectively. We also occasionally see diminished 7th intervals, which are one half step smaller than minor 7ths.

Enharmonic Intervals

You'll notice that both F♯ and G♭ are listed, even though they are the same note. The term for a note having two different names is *enharmonic* (i.e., F♯ and G♭ are enharmonic to each other). Don't get confused by enharmonic intervals. Always remember the rule of the interval's quantity! For an interval to be called a 2nd, there must be *two* note names involved. For an interval to be a 6th, there must be *six* note names involved, etc.

For example, what's the interval from C to E♭? Well, we know it's some kind of 3rd because there are three note names involved: C (1), D (2), and E♭ (3). And we know that it's a *minor* 3rd because it's three half steps in distance (this is confirmed in the chart above).

What about the interval from C to D♯? The notes E♭ and D♯ are enharmonic; they're the same note. But the interval from C to D♯ is technically *not* a minor 3rd. Why? Because of the quantity rule! There are only *two* note names involved: C (1) and D♯ (2). We know that from C to D is a major 2nd, and since C to D♯ is one half step larger than a major 2nd, we call it an *augmented* 2nd. It will sound just like a minor 3rd, and if you heard it, you'd probably call it a minor 3rd, as that label is much more common. But there are instances when it will make sense to write it as C to D♯, instead of C to E♭, and in those instances, it's technically considered an augmented 2nd.

At this point, I'd recommend taking a breather. Take a walk around the block, maybe play a practical joke on your spouse, etc. Then come back and re-read the first part of this chapter before moving on. If anything is still fuzzy, review it before moving on.

HARMONIZING THE MAJOR SCALE

A *chord* is created when three or more notes are sounded together (though a chord can be implied with only two notes, that's technically a *dyad*). When we build chords from each note of a major scale, we say we're *harmonizing* the scale. It's a process that involves a technique called "stacking 3rds." You now know that a 3rd refers to an interval in which three note names are involved. Obviously, we don't often play chords on the bass, but understanding their structure is critical to understanding harmony in general.

The most common chord in popular music is a *triad*, which contains three different notes. We can build a triad by stacking two 3rd intervals from a major scale. We'll work in the key of C major again for starters.

Let's say we want to build a triad from the tonic of this scale, C. Our first note of the chord is going to be the root note, which is C.

For the next note, we're going to stack a 3rd on top of that. Just count up the musical alphabet through the notes of the C major scale: C (1)–D (2)–**E (3)**. A 3rd above C is E.

And now we need to stack another 3rd on top of that to get the last note: E (1)–F (2)–**G (3)**. A 3rd above E is G.

So, the triad built from the first degree of our C major scale is spelled C–E–G. This is a C major triad.

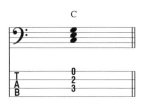

Chord Symbols

Notice the "C" above the music in the last example. This is a chord symbol, and it indicates the present harmony. Normally, these are literally interpreted by guitarists, keyboardists, etc., but we as bassists need to be familiar with their meaning in order to generate appropriate bass lines. A chord symbol like this—with only a capital letter—always indicates a major triad. So "C" stands for a C major chord (C–E–G).

When the symbol contains a lowercase "m" after it, it stands for a minor triad. So "Dm" stands for a D minor chord (D–F–A).

Another way to look at this triad is as two different intervals measured from the root note: C to E is a major 3rd (four half steps), and C to G is a perfect 5th (seven half steps). Knowing this, we can say that the formula for a major triad is: root–major 3rd–perfect 5th. This formula holds true for *any* major triad.

Now let's build a minor triad from the second degree of our C major scale, D. If we continue the process of stacking 3rds, now from the note D, we get D–F–A. This is a D minor triad.

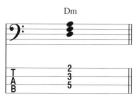

When we measure the two different intervals from the root of a minor triad, we discover that the formula is different than the major triad. D to F is a *minor* 3rd (three half steps), and D to A is a perfect 5th (seven half steps). So, the formula for a minor triad is root–minor 3rd–perfect 5th. Compared to a major triad, the only difference is that the 3rd has been lowered a half step.

Continuing on with the process, we end up with several more major and minor triads from the C major scale: Em, F, G, and Am.

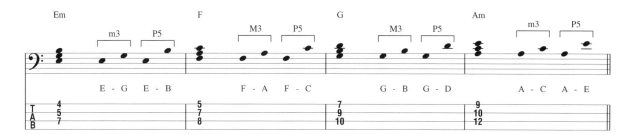

Remember: Since we're harmonizing the C major scale, we're just using notes from that scale here (C–D–E–F–G–A–B). We stopped before we reached the last note, B, for a reason. The chord we get here is a *diminished* triad. The formula for a diminished triad is root–minor 3rd–diminished 5th. It's close to a minor triad, but the 5th has been lowered by a half step. This makes quite a bit of difference in the sound, as you'll hear. The chord symbol for diminished is °.

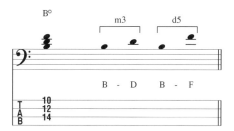

We use Roman numerals to indicate these chords within a key—uppercase for major chords, lowercase for minor, and lowercase plus the ° symbol for diminished. Here are all the triads in the key of C and their corresponding Roman numerals. These would sound pretty muddy on bass if played as chords, so on the audio, you'll hear the chords played on a piano (an octave higher for clarity), and then the bass will echo each by arpeggiating the chords (i.e., playing through the chord tones one note at a time).

Harmonized C Major Scale

TRACK 19

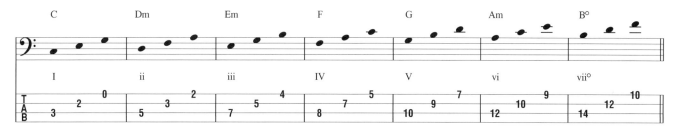

Like our W–W–H–W–W–W–H formula for the major scale that we learned in Chapter 1, this is another formula that's applicable in any key. The diatonic triads for any major key will always follow this pattern: major (I), minor (ii), minor (iii), major (IV), major (V), minor (vi), and diminished (vii°).

So, if you noticed, by harmonizing the major scale, we end up with three types of triads: major, minor, and diminished. Let's compare them all with a C root note, so we can see how notes are altered to create each type. First we have the C major triad:

To make this a C minor triad, we just lower the 3rd, E, by one half step to E♭:

For a C° triad, we have a lowered 3rd (E♭) and a lowered 5th (G♭):

There's also one more type of triad, but we haven't seen it yet because it doesn't occur within the harmonized major scale. It's called an *augmented* triad, and it's spelled 1–3–♯5. It's like a major triad with a raised 5th. The chord symbol for an augmented chord is a capital letter with a "+" sign. Here's C+:

Since it doesn't occur within the harmonized major scale, the augmented triad is *non-diatonic* to a major key. As is expected, they're not as commonly heard as the other diatonic harmonies, but you do come across them occasionally—even in pop music. If you harmonize the harmonic minor scale, which we'll look at on page 24, you'll find an augmented chord. Try it for extra credit!

The degrees of the major scale (and their harmonized triads) have labels that you'll hear—some more often than others:

1. **Tonic:** Home base (same as the key).

2. **Supertonic:** second scale degree (directly "above" the tonic).

3. **Mediant:** third scale degree ("middle" note of the tonic triad).

4. **Subdominant:** fourth scale degree (directly "below" the dominant).

5. **Dominant:** fifth scale degree (the most "dominant" harmonic note after the tonic).

6. **Submediant:** sixth scale degree (the "middle" note of the subdominant triad).

7. **Leading tone:** seventh scale degree (the note that "leads" to the tonic—also referred to as "subtonic").

KEY SIGNATURES

We use *key signatures* to avoid having to constantly write a bunch of sharps or flats (collectively known as *accidentals*) when playing in keys other than C major. It's a group of sharps or flats that appears on the staff at the beginning of a piece, telling the performer to play those notes sharp or flat throughout. Since there are 12 different notes, there are 12 different major keys; hence, there are 12 different key signatures.

By using our W–W–H–W–W–W–H major scale formula and starting on a root note other than C, we soon discover that we need to employ sharps or flats in order to build other major scales. When building any major scale, you can follow these steps: First, write out the seven note names, starting with the tonic. If we want to build a G major scale, for example, we start by writing out the seven note names, starting from G:

$$G–A–B–C–D–E–F$$

Next, we check these notes against the major scale formula. In other words, in order for these notes to form a G major scale, they need to match the pattern of whole and half steps indicated in our formula. A piano keyboard is particularly helpful in this regard because the sharp/flat keys are black.

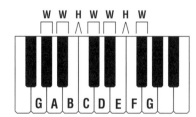

We can see that the formula is all good until the end. From E to F is a half step, and from F to G is a whole step. This conflicts with our formula. So, we raise the F note to F♯, thereby creating the proper intervals.

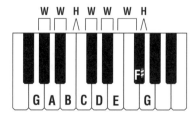

So, we say the key signature for G major is one sharp: F♯. (Looking at a piano keyboard also reveals why C major has a blank key signature: There are naturally occurring half steps between E and F and between B and C.)

Let's try another one. If we build a major scale from the root F, we encounter another problem.

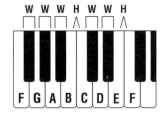

Instead of W–W–H in the beginning, we have W–W–W. We can fix this by lowering B to B♭, thereby adhering to our major scale formula.

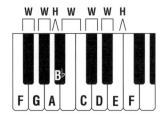

So, the key signature for F major is one flat: B♭. As this demonstrates, we have sharp keys and flat keys (and C major, which is neither). If we repeat this process for each of the 12 different notes, the resultant key signatures will be:

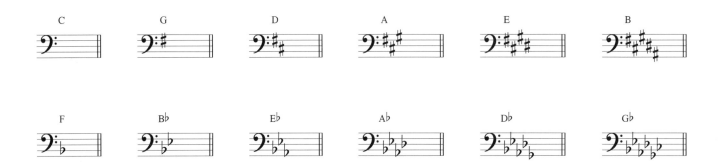

CIRCLE OF 5THS

These 12 key signatures are grouped into a diagram called the *Circle of 5ths*, which helps demonstrate their relationship to each other and makes the process of memorizing them easier. The keys are arranged so that, when progressing clockwise, each key is a 5th higher than the previous one. In other words, from C to G is a 5th: **C** (1)–D (2)–E (3)–F (4)–**G** (5). And from G to D is a 5th: **G** (1)–A (2)–B (3)–C (4)–**D** (5). And so on.

If you look closely, there's a method to the circle's organization. Notice that, when moving to the right (the "sharps" side), each new key contains the same sharps as the previous key plus one more. Moving to the left (the "flats" side) works the same way. Keep this in mind when learning each new key signature. The parentheses indicate each major key's *relative minor* key. Relative major and minor keys contain the same key signature; they just start and end on different notes. The chords used in a song will usually let you know whether the song is in a major key or its relative minor key. For instance, if the key signature is one sharp (F♯), the song could be in G major or E minor. If the song begins and ends on Em, it's a sure bet that the song is in E minor. We'll talk a bit more about this later on.

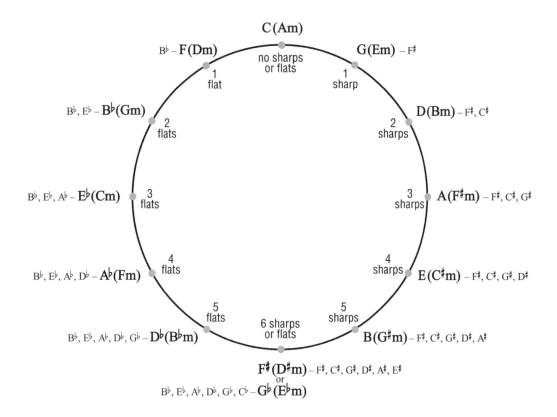

HARMONIZING THE MINOR SCALE

Just as we harmonized the major scale, we can do the same for the minor scale. We simply stack a diatonic 3rd and 5th over each degree of the scale. Let's do this with an A minor scale, which, as demonstrated by our Circle of 5ths diagram, contains the same notes as the C major scale; it just treats A as the root instead of C. Here's what we'll get:

TRACK 24

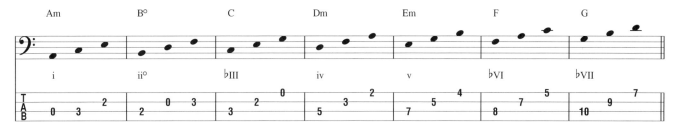

Notice that this is the same exact set of chords that we got when we harmonized the C major scale, only we're starting from Am, and the Roman-numeral analysis is reflecting that. Compare the Roman numerals to the 1–2–♭3–4–5–♭6–♭7 minor scale numeric formula we discussed in Chapter 1, and you should see the relationship. We're still using uppercase for major chords and lowercase for minor chords, but the numerals have changed because the tonic is now A instead of C.

Just as with the major scale, there's a diatonic minor-key chord formula for every minor key: minor (i), diminished (ii°), major (♭III), minor (iv), minor (v), major (♭VI), major (♭VII).

The V Chord

In minor keys, an exception when dealing with the V chord occurs so commonly that it's really more of a rule. Notice that the diatonic v chord in the key of A minor is normally Em (v). The problem with this is that it doesn't result in a very strong resolution to the tonic i chord (Am) because it lacks a *leading tone*—a note that's one half step below the tonic.

When we play the V chord in C major, which is a G chord, the 3rd of the chord (B) is the leading tone of the key; in other words, it's one half step below C. This note pulls the ear toward the tonic, resulting is a strong resolution. However, in A minor, the 3rd of the v chord (Em) is G, which is one *whole step* below the tonic A. This one detail makes quite a difference, as you'll soon hear.

So, in minor keys, we often replace the minor v chord with a major V chord, thereby raising the 3rd (in our case, G) by one half step (G♯) and creating the leading tone necessary for strong resolution. Listen to the following example, played on piano, to hear the difference this makes.

TRACK 25

The former is heard in some folk music that draws heavily from modal sounds (modes are covered in Chapters 6–9), but the latter is what we often hear in most rock, pop, jazz, classical, etc. When we raise this note a half step, a new scale is created, which is called the *harmonic minor scale*. It's like a minor scale, but with a raised seventh degree. Its numeric formula, then, is: 1–2–♭3–4–5–♭6–7.

A Harmonic Minor

Here's a fingering shape for A harmonic minor based mostly around fifth position. Notice its similarity to Shape 2 of the minor scale from Chapter 1.

A Harmonic Minor

TRACK 26

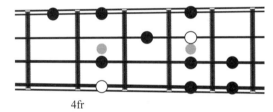

4fr

We'll touch more on the harmonic minor scale and its applications later. For now, just remember that in minor keys, the minor v chord is often changed to a major V chord to provide stronger resolution to the tonic.

Well, that's plenty of theory for now. If your brain is still in one piece, go grab a beverage and relax. You may want to re-read this chapter when you feel up to it to make sure that you're grasping all the concepts. Now it's time to get down with some lines.

WHAT YOU LEARNED:

- **Interval qualities** (major, minor, perfect, augmented, and diminished) and **quantities** (2nd, 3rd, etc.).
- The term **enharmonic**: the same note spelled two different ways (for instance, F♯ and G♭).
- Several fingering patterns for major and major pentatonic scales.
- The harmonization of the major and minor scales.
- Four types of **triads** (major: 1–3–5, minor: 1–♭3–5, diminished: 1–♭3–♭5, and augmented: 1–3–♯5).
- **Key signatures** and the **Circle of 5ths**.

CHAPTER 3: FILLING IN THE GAPS WITH CHORD TONES

It's time to begin putting our new knowledge to work on some bass lines. In this chapter, we'll start using chord tones, other than the root, to add a bit of variety to our lines. Before starting this chapter, make sure that you're clear on the "What You Learned" summaries from Chapters 1 and 2.

THE 5TH

One of the most common non-root chord tones used in bass lines is the 5th. It's a simple device, but oftentimes it can be just what's needed to provide some motion. You already know how to play 5th intervals on the bass, even if you don't realize it yet. The interval shapes were hidden in the scales and chord (arpeggio) shapes of Chapters 1 and 2. I won't make you go back and search, though. We'll just review them quickly.

The great thing about learning intervals on the bass is that the strings are all tuned in 4ths, which means an interval looks the same no matter which strings you're using. For example, we can play a perfect 5th interval basically two different ways on the bass: on adjacent strings or on non-adjacent strings. But either method looks the same on any string set. Take a look (in the following diagrams, "R" stands for "root," and "5" stands for "5th"):

Perfect 5ths – Adjacent Strings

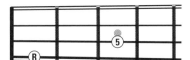 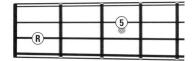 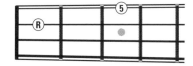

Perfect 5ths – Non-Adjacent Strings

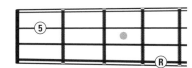 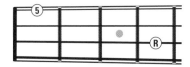

If you'll remember, there's one more type of 5th that occurs in a diatonic major scale: the diminished 5th, from the diminished triad. The non-adjacent version of this interval is a bit of stretch, so it's not nearly as commonly used as the adjacent one, but we'll include it for the sake of being thorough.

Diminished 5ths – Adjacent Strings

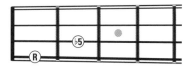 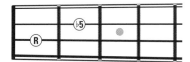 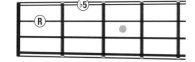

Diminished 5ths – Non-Adjacent Strings

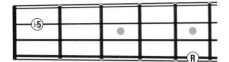 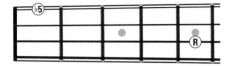

What this means is that, anytime you're playing under a major or minor chord (which has a perfect 5th in it), you can decorate your bass line with that chord's 5th, as well. When playing over a diminished chord (much rarer, but it does occur occasionally), you can decorate your line with the ♭5th. So let's check out some lines to see this idea in action. These examples will use nothing but each chord's root and/or 5th. In the real world, there's no reason to be so exclusive with our note choices, but this helps to demonstrate just how much a single note can help to liven things up a bit.

Function, Function, Function

Notice that the Roman-numeral analysis is also provided here. I want you to really be thinking about each chord's function within the key and start making the auditory connection in this regard. This is extremely good ear training. Eventually, you'll be able to listen to a song and know when you're hearing the IV chord or ii chord without having to even pick up your instrument. It just takes practice and conscious listening.

First, start by identifying if the chord sounds major or minor. This is usually fairly easy for most people. Then, you need to identify which major or minor chord it is. The I chord will feel like home. The V chord will feel as though it needs to resolve. This is because it contains the leading tone and does not contain the tonic of the key. The IV chord will sound more resolved than the V but not as much as the I chord.

The vi chord will sound like the most resolved minor chord of the song because it shares two notes with the I chord. The ii chord will have a similar effect as the IV chord because it shares two notes with it. The same connection is present between the iii chord and the V chord. The more you are aware of these harmonic traits, the better you'll become at recognizing them.

If you have a keyboard handy, practice playing simple triads in the key of C (it's all white keys, so it's the easiest). If you don't have one handy, at least listen to Track 19 (the harmonized C major scale) for practice. Tracks 20–23 are also great practice for identifying the sounds of the four different triads from the same root.

Example 1 uses a simple I–vi chord progression in C major: C–Am. This is just about as simple as it gets, but the 5th (the G note over the C chord) really helps to connect the two harmonies.

Example 1

TRACK 27

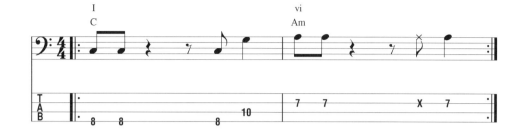

In Example 2, which is in A minor, we're using the root and 5th of each chord to create a motive. Ideas like this can become miniature "hooks" in their own right.

Example 2

TRACK 28

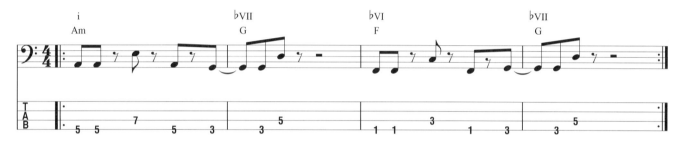

We'll move into some other keys now. Refer to the Circle of 5ths diagram if you're curious about the key signatures, and look back at the neck diagram on page 14 if you're having trouble remembering the note names (there's also a full neck diagram in Appendix A). Example 3 is a reggae-style line in Gm—specifically, a i–♭III (Gm–B♭) progression. We're including both the octave and the 5th here to create another motive. If you're unfamiliar with it, the octave shape is illustrated below. Coincidentally, once you learn the notes on strings 4 and 3, octaves are a great way to learn them on strings 2 and 1.

Example 3

TRACK 29

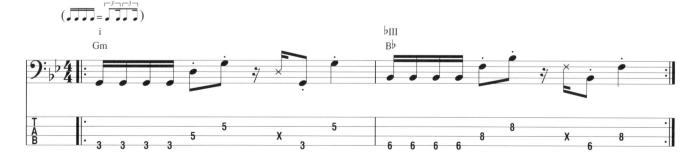

Simply alternating the root and 5th with a catchy rhythm works great in many instances, as demonstrated in the D major progression of Example 4.

Example 4

TRACK 30

We can also play the 5th that lies below the chord's root. This note simply lies on the same fret as the root, one string below. (**Note:** When we say "one string below," we're talking in terms of pitch—not physical location. The lowest string is string 4 [the thickest], and the highest is string 1 [the thinnest].)

Alternating the root with the 5th below it is very popular in country styles. Example 5 demonstrates a typical example in the key of C. For the I (C) and IV (F) chords, we're alternating with the low 5th. For the V (G) chord, we use the higher 5th. You can mix and match the upper and lower 5ths pretty much at your discretion, especially when playing slower lines such as these.

Example 5

TRACK 31

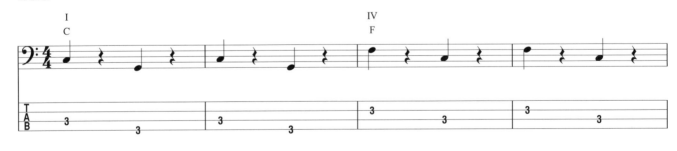

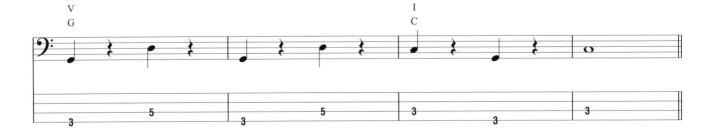

There's also another interesting way to use the chord's 5th. Rather than alternate it with the root, sometimes you can just play the 5th instead. One common place to do this is when you have a I–V–I move, as is the case with this example in E major. After climbing I (E)–ii (F♯m)–IV (A), we have the I–V (B)–I move. Here, we simply play B notes for the I and V chords, where it functions as the 5th of the I chord and the root of the V chord. We then resolve to the root (E) for the final I chord. This is technically known as an *inversion*, which is a concept that we'll explore later on. The chord symbol for this chord, "E/B," is called a *slash chord* and is read as "E over B"—in other words, an E major chord over a B bass note.

Example 6

TRACK 32

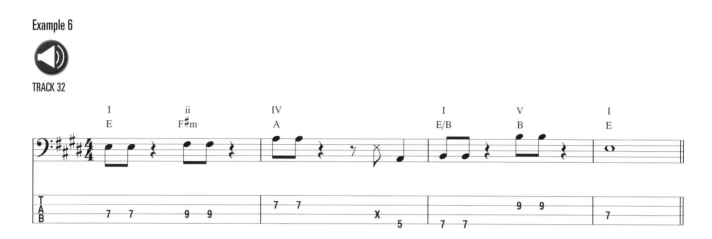

Here's an example in B minor, which uses the major V chord (in this case, F♯) that we learned about in Chapter 2. This won't make much of a difference in our bass lines right now, since we're only using the root and 5th of each chord (remember: it's the *3rd* of the V chord that's changed in order to make it major). But you'll hear its effect in the chords played by the other instruments. When we start adding other notes to our lines, this change will affect what we play. Notice that we're also bringing the octave root notes into play here.

Example 7

TRACK 33

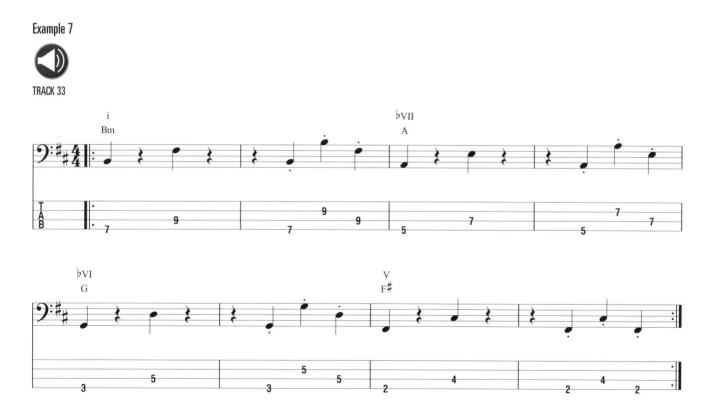

THE 3RD

Besides the 5th, the other triad chord tone that we have available to us is the 3rd. There are two kinds of 3rds: major (four half steps) and minor (three half steps). The only practical way to play these intervals (harmonically, that is) is on adjacent strings. Let's check out the shapes.

Major 3rds

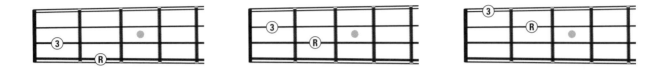

Minor 3rds

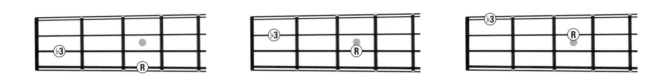

So, anytime you're playing under a major chord, you can use the major 3rd, as well. If you're playing under a minor chord, you can use the minor 3rd. Let's take a look at some examples using only the roots and 3rds (major or minor) of each chord.

Here's an example in C that moves from I (C) to IV (F). We use the major 3rd of the C chord (E) as a connecting tone that leads to F.

Example 8

TRACK 34

This example in E uses the 3rds of the I and IV chords in connecting fashion, as well.

Example 9

TRACK 35

Here's a rockin' line in G minor that's played with a pick. We're using 3rds for the tonic (Gm) and ♭VI chords to provide some motion and momentum to the line.

Example 10

TRACK 36

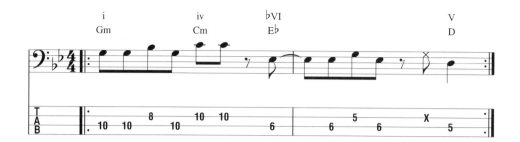

ARPEGGIOS

You've now learned how to add the 3rd and 5th chord tones to your bass lines. When you incorporate both options together, you're entering the world of arpeggios. As mentioned earlier, an *arpeggio* is simply the notes of a chord played one at a time instead of all together. Bassists can use arpeggios to imply the harmony even when no other rhythm instruments are playing (a common example of this is a blues trio in which the guitarist is playing a solo).

So let's look at some common arpeggio shapes for our four different types of triads: major, minor, diminished, and augmented. Just as with scales, arpeggios also have numeric formulas in which the degrees are numbered, with the major scale being the standard. So, a major arpeggio's formula is 1–3–5, since it contains a root, major 3rd, and a perfect 5th. The formula for each arpeggio is given below. These will all span one octave—in other words, root–3rd–5th–root. (**Note:** There are certainly other ways to play these arpeggios, and we'll examine some of those later on, but these are good beginning fingerings. You'll find a more comprehensive set of arpeggio fingerings in Appendix A.)

Major Arpeggios (1–3–5)

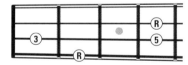　　　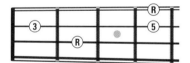

Minor Arpeggios (1–♭3–5)

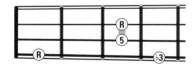　　　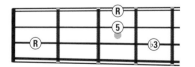

Diminished Arpeggios (1–♭3–♭5)

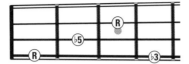 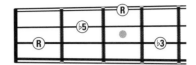

Augmented Arpeggios (1–3–♯5)

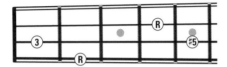 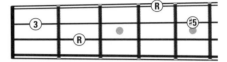

So, just as before with the 3rd and the 5th, any time you're playing under a major chord, you can make use of the major arpeggio, and likewise with the minor arpeggios for minor chords. Again, we won't find any augmented arpeggios at this point, because we're only dealing with chords diatonic to the major scale, which doesn't contain an augmented chord. Diminished triads are also quite rare, even though they are diatonic to the major scale.

Let's check out some lines that make use of these arpeggio shapes. Here's an example of a 12-bar blues progression in A, which uses the I, IV, and V chords. Blues music often uses seventh chords, which we'll look at in Chapter 10, but this style of blues, known as a *rhumba blues*, sounds great with triads, too. In this format, major arpeggios are commonly applied to each chord for a catchy rhythm.

Example 11

TRACK 37

Here's an example in E minor using a i–♭VI–V progression. Note the major V chord in the minor key. Appropriately, we play the notes of a B major arpeggio (B–D♯–F♯) for this chord. Also notice how we use the Em chord's low 5th (B) to smoothly lead into the C chord. This example does a good job of demonstrating how you don't need to play the notes of an arpeggio straight through (up or down); you can mix them up, too, as evidenced under the B chord (measure 4).

Example 12

TRACK 38

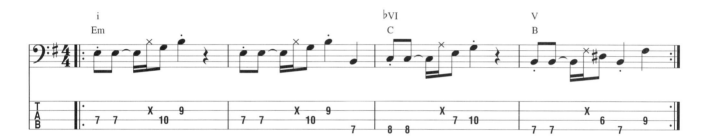

This example in F shows how you can really get creative with arpeggios. For the first F chord, we start with the root but then jumble up the 5th and 3rd. For the C chord, we start with the 5th (G) and descend through the 3rd to get to the root. For the B♭ chord, we travel straight up through the three tones (B♭, D, and F); however, for the F chord in measure 4, we jumble up the notes again: 3rd, 5th, and root. In this way, the bass can add a melodic component to the proceedings, as well.

Example 13

TRACK 39

Here's a line in C# minor that uses arpeggio shapes based off the third string. We use the same rhythmic idea for both arpeggios: C#m and B. This is great for academic purposes because we get to see the adaptation of a minor arpeggio shape for a major arpeggio shape. Remember, however, that just because you use arpeggios for one chord doesn't mean that you have to use them for each. Another nice version of this line, for instance, would involve simply leaving measure 4 completely blank.

Example 14

TRACK 40

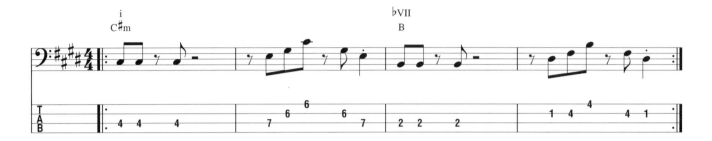

WHAT YOU LEARNED:

- **Interval shapes:** perfect 5th, diminished 5th, major 3rd, minor 3rd, octave.

- Decorating root-note bass lines with the 5th or the 3rd.

- **One-octave arpeggio shapes:** major, minor, diminished, and augmented.

- Creating bass lines with arpeggios for diatonic major and minor chords.

CHAPTER 4: FILLING IN THE GAPS WITH SCALE TONES

In the previous chapter, we learned how to use a chord's 3rd and/or 5th to generate some alternative ideas to just plugging away on root notes. Even with only these added notes, the possibilities are vastly increased when you also consider the rhythm, order of notes, repetition of notes, etc. However, the approach is still limited, as you're stuck with just three different notes for each chord.

In this chapter, we'll take a look at how we can access other notes from the diatonic scale to further shake things up in our bass lines. If chord tones are the foundation and framing of our harmonic house, other scale tones can be thought of as the trim, paint colors, cabinetry, or flooring—the decorative touches—that can really give each dwelling its own distinct personality.

Determining the Key

The first thing we need to know before we can start using other scale tones in our lines is the key of the song. This is easy if we have the music in front of us, but what if we don't have sheet music? How do we know the key of the song without a key signature?

The first thing to try is to use your ear. Hum along with the song and see if you can tell what note sounds like the tonic, or the most resolved. This is often the last note of a melody (think of "Twinkle, Twinkle, Little Star," for instance) or the final chord of a song. If you think you've located the tonic with this method, play the major scale along with the song to see if it sounds right. Does it sound way wrong? Maybe the song is in a minor key. Try playing the minor scale from that note.

If neither of these methods work, but you know the chords to the song, you can determine the key by process of elimination. If a song has four chords in it—say, F, B♭, Dm, and C—you can plug those chords into different keys to see if they fit our harmonized major scale formula: I–ii–iii–IV–V–vi–vii°. Write out that formula and then plug in the chords in three rows below it, treating each chord as the tonic, or I chord (remember: F and D minor are relative to each other, so the chords contained in their keys would be the same). It will look like this:

	I	ii	iii	IV	V	vi	vii°
Key of F	F			B♭	C	Dm	
Key of B♭	B♭	X	Dm		F		
Key of C	C	Dm		F			X

After you cross out chords that don't fit the formula, you'll usually be left with only one choice. If we treat B♭ as the tonic, for example, we see that C is in the ii chord spot. The key of B♭ should have a Cm chord, though, so that's not right. The key of C works except for the B♭ chord, so that's wrong, as well. In this instance, the key is most likely F major. The fewer chords there are in a song, the harder it can be to determine the key. But with this formula, combined with the ear approach mentioned above, you should be able to figure it out.

Once you know the key, it's a simple task of using the appropriate major or minor scale to create lines. If the song is in the key of G major, for example, you'd use the G major scale (or G major pentatonic) from which to draw your extra scale tones. If it were in G minor, you'd use the G minor scale (or G minor pentatonic). This is sometimes referred to as the *key center* approach to improvising. Let's take a look at some examples that do just that.

MAJOR SCALE EXAMPLES

This first example demonstrates an extremely common application of this technique: connecting tones. We have a simple I–vi–IV–V progression in C major, and we use the in-between scale tones to connect the chords. For the G chord, since we have to move up a 4th to C (for the repeat), we use eighth and quarter notes to travel through A and B. We're working out of Shape 2 of the C major scale form here.

Example 1

TRACK 41

Another very common device—especially in Motown and R&B styles—is to use the major pentatonic scale based on each major chord. In this D major example that moves from I (D) to IV (G), we play D major pentatonic notes for the D chord and G major pentatonic notes for the G chord to create a memorable little line. Check out the '60s hit "Sugar Pie, Honey Bunch" to hear this idea in action. John Paul Jones's beautiful line at the beginning of Zeppelin's "Ramble On" is another classic example of pentatonic riffery. We're using Shape 3 of the major pentatonic scale for the D chord here and Shape 4 for the G chord.

Example 2

TRACK 42

The previous example also brings to light a good rule: any time you're playing over a diatonic major chord (whether in a major or minor key), you can use the *major pentatonic* scale based on that chord (not the full major scale, though!), because all five of those notes will be diatonic to the scale. For example, in the key of D, we have three major chords: I (D), IV (G), and V (A). Of course, we can use D major pentatonic, because it's the same as the D major scale, only with two notes omitted. G major pentatonic contains G–A–B–D–E, which are all diatonic to D major. And A major pentatonic contains A–B–C♯–E–F♯, which are all diatonic to D major, as well. So, matching major pentatonics and major chords are all fair game when creating your lines. But only one major scale (i.e., the key of the song) will work.

Consequently, the same rule applies to minor chords and their matching minor pentatonic scales. So, for example, in the key of D, you also have three minor chords: ii (Em), iii (F♯m), and vi (Bm). Over each of those chords, you could use their respective minor pentatonic scale, as well, because all of the tones are diatonic to D major (or the relative minor, B minor). Again, though, only one full minor scale (B minor) will work.

Note that when I say "will work," I mean that it will be the only minor scale that doesn't contain any non-diatonic notes. But there are certainly times when you'll need to use non-diatonic notes—or even times when you'll choose to do so just for the effect. We'll look at those instances a bit later. For now, we're just playing things "by the book," so to speak (i.e., learning the rules before we break them).

Here's a hard-rocking example in B minor played with a pick. We're working out of Shape 1 of the B minor scale here (second position). This approach represents kind of a combination of the connecting tones and melodic riff strategies. For Bm, we're using neighboring tones to provide a bit of movement leading into the D chord. Over the D chord, we play a melodic riff that leads dramatically down to the G chord via a leap of a 5th, from D to G. And for the G chord in measure 4, we see another common device—alternating between the root and a neighbor tone—which is kind of nice for "treading water" until you're ready to move somewhere else.

Example 3

TRACK 43

Sometimes, when songs hang on only one chord for a long time, you can take a bit of liberty and create a riff of your own to keep things interesting. You may not want to do this if there are already lots of busy parts going on, but if there's plenty of space available, a nice riff may be just what the doctor ordered. Here's an example of that in C minor. The guitar and keys are playing mostly sustained chords, so we can get a little busy with a riff from C minor pentatonic if we'd like. This one comes from Shape 3 of the C minor pentatonic scale (fifth position).

Example 4

TRACK 44

Remember that the root is still supreme, with the other chord tones (3rd and 5th) second in terms of harmonic weight. So, unless you're taking a solo, don't forget that your primary job is still to provide the harmonic anchor. But there's quite a disparity between playing a solo and playing nothing but root notes, and in-between those two extremes lies plenty of opportunity for creative lines.

WHAT YOU LEARNED:

- **How to determine the key of a song** when you don't have the sheet music.

- The **pentatonic rule:** you can use the matching major or minor pentatonic scale over a major or minor chord.

- How to use scale tones to **connect the roots of each chord.**

- How to use scale tones to **create melodies or riffs** in order to give a line movement or direction.

CHAPTER 5: INVERSIONS AND SLASH CHORDS

We briefly mentioned the concepts of inversions and slash chords in Chapter 3; now we're going to look at them more closely, as they can be one of the most powerful tools for a bassist when used appropriately. Players like Paul McCartney, James Jamerson, and John Paul Jones made extensive use of inversions to great effect in many of their lines. In many instances, these lines form the most memorable hooks of the song (or at least a section of the song).

WHAT IS AN INVERSION?

So what's an inversion, anyway? Simply put, it's a chord that contains a chord tone other than the root in the bottom. Guitarists and keyboardists can voice their chords so that the 5th or 3rd is the lowest note, and by doing so, they're playing inversions. However, if there's a bass present, it's kind of a moot point with regard to the overall harmony, because the bass has the final word on the bottom end.

There are three different ways we can arrange the notes of a triad:

- **Root position:** the chord's root is on the bottom.
- **First inversion:** the chord's 3rd is on the bottom.
- **Second inversion:** the chord's 5th is on the bottom.

Let's take a look at how we can use arpeggios to arrange a major triad into inversions. The first shape should be familiar to you, as we covered it in Chapter 3. We'll use a C major chord here and work out of seventh position. The chord tones are identified between the staves.

TRACK 45

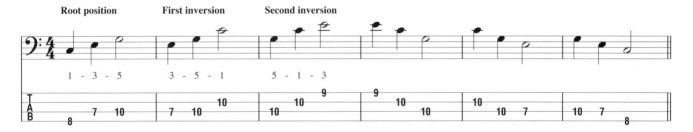

This is not to say, of course, that you have to play arpeggios when using inversions. But I want you to be familiar with the orientation of the other two chord tones when playing a note other than the root. To that end, let's take a look at the most common fingerings for three-note major and minor arpeggios in each arrangement (root position, first inversion, and second inversion).

Major – Root Position

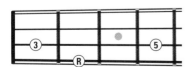

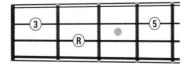

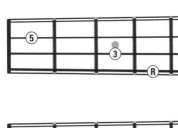
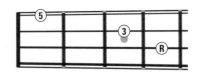

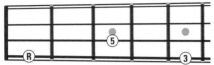
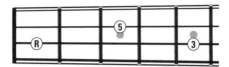

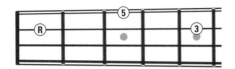

Major – First Inversion

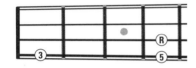
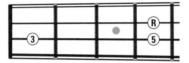

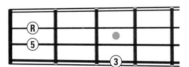

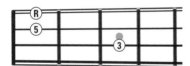

Major – Second Inversion

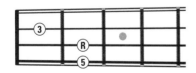
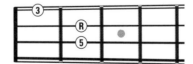

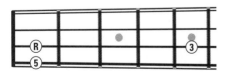
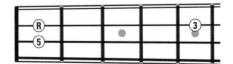

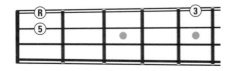

Minor – Root Position

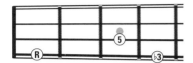
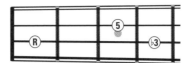

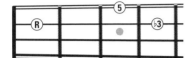
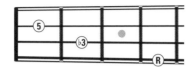

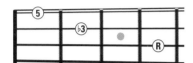
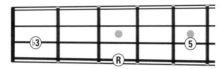

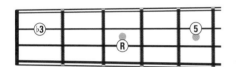
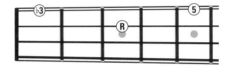

Minor – First Inversion

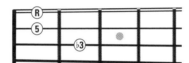

Minor – Second Inversion

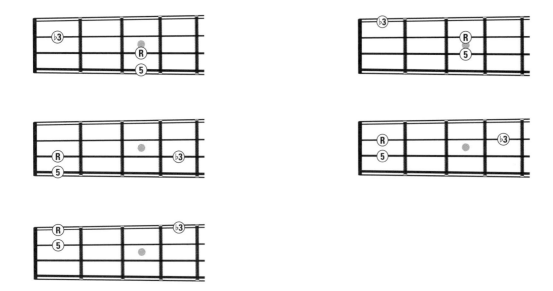

WHAT'S A SLASH CHORD?

A *slash chord* is one that contains a note other than the root in the bottom. Slash chords are represented by chord symbols in which two note names are divided by a slash, such as "C/E" or "F/C." In these instances, the left letter represents the chord, and the right letter represents the bass note. So, the aforementioned slash chords would be read as "C over E" (or "C with an E in the bass") and "F over C" (or "F with a C in the bass"), respectively.

How does this differ from an inversion? Good question. The answer is that sometimes it does and sometimes it doesn't. It's one of those "all squares are rectangles, but not all rectangles are squares" things. In our case, *all inversions are slash chords*, but *not all slash chords are inversions*.

What do we mean by this? Well, let's get specific. We said:

- An inversion is a chord that contains a *chord tone* other than the root in the bottom.
- A slash chord is one that contains a *note* other than the root in the bottom.

Do you see the difference now? The inversion has to contain a chord tone in the bottom, but a slash chord just has to contain a note other than the root in the bottom. This means that a slash chord could contain *any* other note than the root in the bottom. So you could (and do) have chords like C/D, C/F, A/F, etc. Sometimes these chords can also be named without a slash, using extended harmonies. For example, an Em/C chord could also be called Cmaj7 (we'll look at seventh chords in Chapter 10). Sometimes the musical context will determine which name makes more sense. Other times, it's simply a matter of taste.

INVERSION EXAMPLES

Let's listen to some examples that use inversions. You'll probably recognize these sounds, as they're fairly common. This first is in A and uses the classic move of the I chord in root position followed by the I chord in first inversion.

Example 1

TRACK 46

Here's another common device: using the tonic note for both the I and IV chords. This means that the I chord will be in root position, while the IV chord will be in second inversion (its 5th in the bass). This example is in E♭, so that translates to E♭ and A♭/E♭ chords. In order to liven up things a bit, we're incorporating a little embellishment from the E♭ major pentatonic scale and some syncopation.

Example 2

TRACK 47

Note that the harmonic analysis remains the same for the inverted chords because the chord isn't changing; only the bass note is. So, A♭/E♭ is still the IV chord in the key of E♭ even though it has E♭ in the bass.

This next example features two more commonly used inversions—the first-inversion V chord and the second-inversion I chord—in a descending line that makes its way down from I to IV and back up. We're in E major here and are descending the major scale one note at a time to create a combination of root-position and inverted chords.

Example 3

TRACK 48

SLASH-CHORD EXAMPLES

And now let's take a look at some other slash chord examples in which the bass note is not a chord tone. One common application of this is the pedal-bass-tone approach. This is where the bass holds the same note beneath changing chords on top. Here's an example of that approach in F# minor. The harmonies climb from ♭VI (D) to ♭VII (E) and on up to i (F#m), but the bass remains on F# throughout, as if pecking out some low frequency Morse code.

Example 4

TRACK 49

Another common slash chord is the IV chord with the fifth of the scale in the bass. In other words, in the key of G, this would be a C (IV) chord with a D (fifth note of G major scale) in the bass. You hear this in lots of Beatles songs, such as "The Long and Winding Road."

Example 5

TRACK 50

Notice the harmonic analysis for the C/D chord shows "V." This is a bit of a foggy area, as the chord really has its feet in two different worlds: IV and V. It's really functioning more as a suspended dominant chord. A *suspended chord* (or *sus chord*) is one in which the chord's 3rd has been replaced by the 4th (or sometimes the 2nd). So a Dsus4 chord, for example, would contain the notes D (root), G (4th), and A (5th) instead of D (root), F# (3rd), and A (5th).

Oftentimes, the composer of a song will write a specific slash chord, and in those instances, he/she clearly wants a specific sound. However, don't be afraid to experiment with other ideas in this regard. If you find yourself playing over a common progression like I–IV–V or ♭VI–♭VII–i, and you feel as though things are a little stale, try playing a pedal tone on the tonic like we did in Example 4 to create some slash-chord harmonies. The same idea can work great in major keys, too. Of course, it won't always fit, but sometimes it can really make a song come to life.

And you don't have to stop there. The sky is the limit with this stuff. Sometimes a note will just sound great for whatever reason. Try recording some piano chords, playing different bass notes beneath them to hear what it sounds like. If you find something you like, make a note of it so you can remember the formula—for example, "playing a major 2nd on the IV chord" (this is the strategy employed in Example 5).

It's obviously best to do this exploration in the comfort of your own home rather than on the bandstand (if you want to keep your gig, that is). But, if you're in a band and aren't participating in the songwriting, ideas like these can provide a creative outlet, whether they're used or not. Who knows? It may be just what the doctor ordered.

WHAT YOU LEARNED:

- An **inversion** is a chord in which a chord tone other than the root is on bottom.

- Common fingerings for **root-position**, **first-inversion**, and **second-inversion** major and minor triad arpeggios.

- Root position = root on bottom, first inversion = 3rd on bottom, second inversion = 5th on bottom.

- Common methods for employing inversions in bass lines.

- A **slash chord** is one in which a note (any note) other than the root is on bottom.

- In the chord symbol for a slash chord, the left letter represents the chord, and the right letter represents the bass note.

- A **pedal tone** is a repeated tone (often in the bass) amid changing harmonies.

- A **suspended chord** is one in which the 3rd has been replaced by the 4th or 2nd.

- Common applications of slash chords.

CHAPTER 6: THE MODES

Ah, the modes—the subject of much online debate by bassists and guitarists alike (I suppose they may be equally misunderstood by other instrumentalists, too, but bassists and guitarists are notoriously puzzled by them). For a long time, players have looked to modes to expand their options after growing tired of the major and minor scales. This is certainly logical, and it's no coincidence that we're covering modes after the major and minor scales in this book. However, without an understanding of how to apply them, "knowing your modes" isn't going to do much good at all.

TWO WAYS TO VIEW MODES

There are seven traditional modes, and I believe they can be viewed in two ways:

1. **The Relative Method:** seven different ways to play one major scale;

    or

2. **The Parallel Method:** seven different scales in their own right.

These two ways of understanding modes aren't mutually exclusive at all; there are many bits of information that overlap from one method to the other. But, with regard to practical application, the differences are more pronounced. By the way, while "relative" and "parallel" aren't new musical terms, they're not usually applied to the modes in this way. The reason I attach these terms to them is that, in my opinion, it makes the concept of modes easier to understand.

MODES: THE RELATIVE METHOD

We heard the term "relative minor" earlier in the book. In a major key, you can find the relative minor by counting up to the sixth degree of the scale. In C major, this would be A: C (1)–D (2)–E (3)–F (4)–G (5)–**A (6)**. So, we'd say that A minor is the relative minor of C major. Consequently, C is the *relative major* of A minor. Alternatively, you may have heard of the "down three frets" trick. That will get the same result. C is on fret 8 of the sixth string; take 3 away from 8 and you get fret 5, which is A.

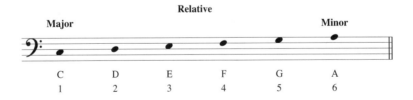

Relative majors and minors share the same key signature and therefore the same set of seven notes; they just have two different tonics. In other words, the key of C contains the notes C–D–E–F–G–A–B; but C major treats C as the tonic, while A minor treats A as the tonic. You can remember this by thinking that they're "relatives" of each other (i.e., from the same "family" of notes).

So how does this relate to modes? Well, the seven modes are just an extension of this concept. If we can treat C or A as the root of this family of notes, what about the other notes? Yep, we can do the same for them—and that's where you get the modes. This is why I call this the "relative method." Since there are seven notes in a major scale, there are seven modes:

1. **Ionian**
2. **Dorian**
3. **Phrygian**
4. **Lydian**
5. **Mixolydian**
6. **Aeolian**
7. **Locrian**

For example, if we were working in the key of C major, we would name these based on each note of the C major scale (C–D–E–F–G–A–B). So the first mode of C major is C Ionian, the second mode of C major is D Dorian, the third mode of C major is E Phrygian, and so on. We can harmonize these modes if we'd like by playing them over the appropriate chord for each degree of the scale, as demonstrated below. For the audio, you'll hear the bass played beneath a keyboard playing the chord.

MODES: THE RELATIVE METHOD

TRACK 51

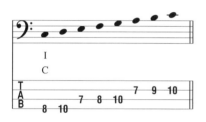

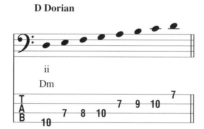

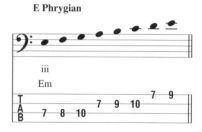

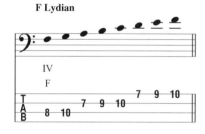

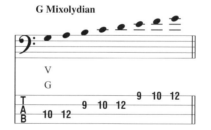

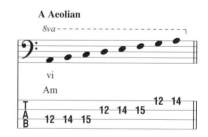

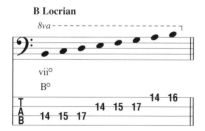

Where Have I Seen You Before?

If you're on top of things, you may have noticed that two of these modes look very familiar: Ionian and Aeolian. There's good reason for this. The Ionian mode is simply another name for the major scale (i.e., C major scale = C Ionian mode), and the Aeolian mode is another name for the minor scale (A minor scale = A Aeolian).

This relationship holds true in any key. If you're in D major, for instance, you find its modes by spelling out the notes of the D major scale (D–E–F#–G–A–B–C#) and playing the scale from each one of those notes, treating each as the root. Here's what you'd get:

D Ionian: D–E–F#–G–A–B–C#

E Dorian: E–F#–G–A–B–C#–D

F# Phrygian: F#–G–A–B–C#–D–E

G Lydian: G–A–B–C#–D–E–F#

A Mixolydian: A–B–C#–D–E–F#–G

B Aeolian: B–C#–D–E–F#–G–A

C# Locrian: C#–D–E–F#–G–A–B

If you were to play all of these as full positional shapes based off the fourth string, you would span an entire octave (12 frets) of the neck:

Modes of D Major

D Ionian

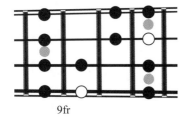

9fr

E Dorian

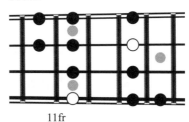

11fr

F# Phrygian

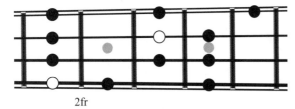

2fr

G Lydian

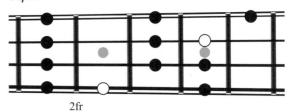

2fr

A Mixolydian

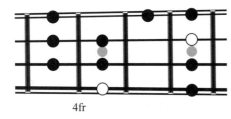

4fr

B Aeolian

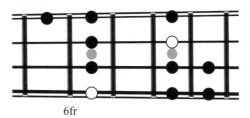

6fr

C# Locrian

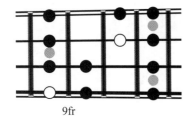

9fr

Another way to view this is simply as the D major scale in seven patterns. That's pretty much all there is to the relative method of thinking about modes. It's a good introduction to modes, but it doesn't teach you much in the way of practical application. Therefore, we need to examine the other side of modes.

A Half-developed Modal Picture

Many players get this far with their modal knowledge and stop. They think, "Oh, OK, I get it! I know all the modes now." But all they really know is fingerings for the major scale all over the neck. Although this is certainly helpful, it's not going to provide any different sounds. If the player is sharp, he or she may intuit that they can play the appropriate mode over its matching chord in a diatonic progression, which is certainly true.

For example, if you have a I–V–vi–IV progression in E major (E–B–C♯m–A), you could play over the progression using the matching mode for each chord: E Ionian over E, B Mixolydian over B, C♯ Aeolian over C♯m, and A Lydian over A.

The problem with this is that it's unnecessarily complicating things. In the end, it's just going to sound like the E major scale; it doesn't matter what scale form you're using. If you're playing over a diatonic major or minor progression such as this, and you only want to use diatonic notes, then there's really no need to involve the modes. You'll use your ear and knowledge of harmony to make the correct note choices.

However, if you're playing over a non-diatonic progression (one in which not all the chords belong to one key), and you need to treat one or more of the chords with a different, specific scale, then you're most likely going to need to call upon a mode or two. This is where the other half of the modal picture comes in.

MODES: THE PARALLEL METHOD

In the parallel method, we're going to look at each mode as a scale in its own right. We learned earlier that the major scale's numeric formula is 1–2–3–4–5–6–7; all other scales can be represented by altering one or more of these numbers (i.e., adding sharps or flats). Now we're going to do the same thing with the modes.

But Modes Aren't Scales! Or Are They?

You'll hear some people go on serious rants about how modes are *not* scales. In my opinion, this is really just a silly matter of semantics. We've already seen evidence of the contrary with two modes: Ionian and Aeolian, also known as the major and minor scales, respectively. So let's get this out of the way right now: yes, modes are scales! Just as the minor scale (Aeolian mode) has a unique numeric scale formula (1–2–♭3–4–5–♭6–♭7) that's different from the major scale, all the other modes have their own unique formulas, too. And that's the essence of the parallel method.

Instead of examining all of the diatonic modes of C major, we're instead going use C as the root note for all the modes. Whereas the relative method looked at the same notes but with different roots, the parallel method looks at the *same root but with different notes*. For each mode, we'll spell the notes and look at a suggested scale shape.

Seven Modes with C as the Root

Ionian mode: 1–2–3–4–5–6–7
C Ionian: C–D–E–F–G–A–B

Construction: As we've already learned, the Ionian mode is simply the major scale. Its formula is the standard by which we judge all other scales, so there are no altered numbers. Its matching diatonic harmony is the major I chord; it's played here in two octaves over a C chord.

Sound and application: The Ionian mode sounds happy and sunny and is the most widely used mode of all, prevalent in almost all forms of pop music, jazz, film scores, classical music, and more.

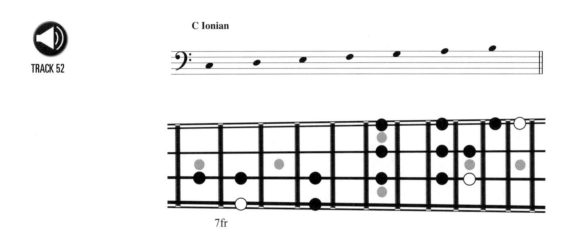

TRACK 52

Dorian mode: 1–2–♭3–4–5–6–♭7
C Dorian: C–D–E♭–F–G–A–B♭

Construction: The Dorian mode can be thought of as a minor scale (Aeolian mode) with a natural 6th degree (instead of the ♭6th). Its matching diatonic harmony is the minor ii chord; it's played here over a Cm chord.

Sound and application: Though it's still a minor mode (due to the ♭3rd degree), Dorian sounds brighter than the Aeolian mode. It's widely used in rock, blues, jazz, pop, and lots of Celtic music, as well.

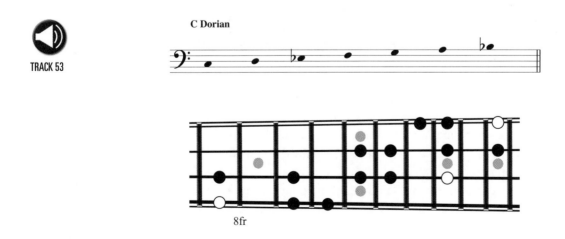

TRACK 53

Phrygian mode: 1–♭2–♭3–4–5–♭6–♭7
C Phrygian: C–D♭–E♭–F–G–A♭–B♭

Construction: The Phrygian mode can be described as a minor scale (Aeolian mode) with a ♭2nd. Its matching diatonic harmony is the minor iii chord; it's played here over a Cm chord.

Sound and application: The ♭2nd degree of Phrygian gives it a slightly exotic sound that's prevalent in some Spanish music and also some metal.

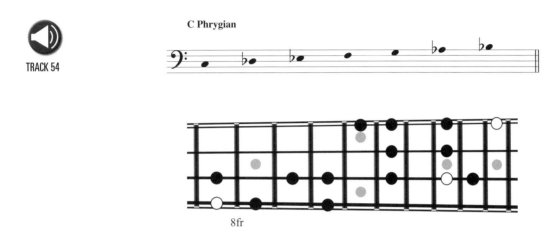

Lydian mode: 1–2–3–♯4–5–6–7
C Lydian: C–D–E–F♯–G–A–B

Construction: The Lydian mode is like a major scale (Ionian mode) with a ♯4th degree. Its matching diatonic harmony is the major IV chord; it's played here over a C major chord.

Sound and application: This is a bright, dreamy-sounding scale that has a mysterious quality to it. You hear it often in jazz and a lot of film scores, as well.

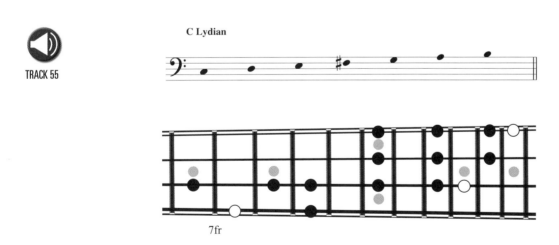

Mixolydian mode: 1–2–3–4–5–6–♭7
C Mixolydian: C–D–E–F–G–A–B♭

Construction: Mixolydian can be thought of as a major scale (Ionian mode) with a ♭7th degree. Its matching diatonic harmony is the major V chord; it's played here over a C major chord.

Sound and application: The Mixolydian mode sounds kind of like a bluesy, funky major scale. It's very common in blues, rock, jazz, and all kinds of pop.

C Mixolydian

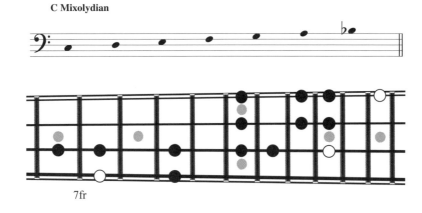

7fr

Aeolian mode: 1–2–♭3–4–5–♭6–♭7
C Aeolian: C–D–E♭–F–G–A♭–B♭

Construction: The Aeolian mode is the same thing as the natural minor scale. Compared to the major scale, it has lowered third, sixth, and seventh degrees. Its matching diatonic harmony is the minor vi chord; it's played here over a Cm chord.

Sound and application: The Aeolian mode sounds dark, sad, and sometimes gothic. You hear it in lots of pop music, rock, metal, some jazz, classical music, and film scores.

C Aeolian

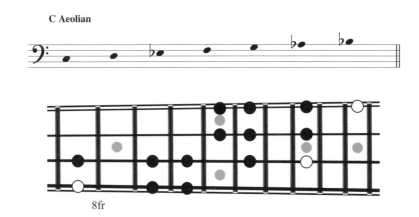

8fr

Locrian mode: 1–♭2–♭3–4–♭5–♭6–♭7
C Locrian: C–D♭–E♭–F–G♭–A♭–B♭

Construction: The Locrian mode is like the Aeolian mode with a ♭2nd and ♭5th. Its matching diatonic harmony is the diminished vii° chord; it's played here over a C° chord.

Sound and application: The ♭5th degree of this mode makes it very unstable. In fact, its matching harmony is a diminished chord—not exactly the pillar of resolution. Outside of jazz, the Locrian mode sees some action in certain metal genres, but that's about it.

C Locrian

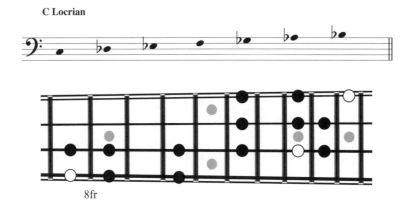

8fr

Major/Minor Distinction

These modes can be roughly broken down into one of two groups: major-sounding or minor-sounding. The determining factor is the 3rd degree.

Major modes:

Ionian

Lydian

Mixolydian

Minor modes:

Dorian

Phrygian

Aeolian

Locrian*

*Technically, Locrian isn't a minor mode since it also contains a ♭5th, which makes its root chord diminished. But for our purposes, the minor label will suffice.

At this point, all you really need to take from this is that you normally play a mode over the appropriate chord type. For example, over a C chord, you may play C Ionian, C Lydian, or C Mixolydian; over a Cm chord, you may play C Dorian, C Phrygian, or C Aeolian; over C°, you would play C Locrian. There are a few factors that would help in determining which mode would be most appropriate, and that's what we'll look at in the next chapter.

WHAT YOU LEARNED:

- Names and fingerings of the seven modes: Ionian, Dorian, Phrygian, Lydian, Mixolydian, Aeolian, Locrian.
- Two modal relationships: **relative** and **parallel**.
- Modes are scales!
- Numeric scalar formula for each mode.
- Modes can be grouped as either **major** or **minor**.

Learn That Neck!

At this point, jump ahead to the appendix and take a look at the remaining scale forms for the major and minor scales and the pentatonic versions of each. The examples in the remainder of this book, though usually based on one form, will begin to freely move through others, so familiarize yourself with all the forms and work on playing them all over the neck. We still have a lot of ground to cover, so I have to trust you to do a little of this legwork on your own!

CHAPTER 7: MODAL APPLICATIONS PART 1— ONE-CHORD VAMPS

Now that we've gotten a grasp on the modes, let's get down to making some music with them. In this chapter, we're going to learn how to choose the right mode(s) to play over a chord that doesn't clearly fit into a diatonic set of harmonies.

If you're in the key of C, and you have C, F, G, and Dm chords, that's no problem. All those chords are diatonic to the key of C. Therefore, the C major scale and/or C major pentatonic scale will sound great. However, what if you just have a one-chord vamp? What do you play over that? Depending on the situation, you could have several options, and that's the subject of this chapter.

WHAT'S A VAMP AND WHAT DO WE DO WITH IT?

A *vamp* is a slang term that basically refers to a section of music that's repeated for as long as necessary. Occasionally, you have a song or a solo section that consists of nothing but one chord. It could be E, A7, Dm7, Bmaj7, or whatever. But that's it. That's all you have to work with—just one chord. How do you determine what you should play over it? There are a few simple steps that will help point you in the right direction.

The Ear Is the Final Judge

It's important to realize that there are no hard-and-fast rules in music. You're not going to be arrested if you choose to play the C major scale over a Cm chord (you may not be hired for another gig, but … that's neither here nor there). All of these concepts that we're discussing are really just conventions; they're what *most* people play *most* of the time because *most* people agree that they sound good.

Our C major scale over a Cm chord example seems blatantly wrong to most people, but not all situations are that cut-and-dried (and, believe it or not, even that specific application can be made to work if done carefully and in the proper context). There will be many times when more than one scale choice would "work," and it's in those instances where your ear, among other possible factors, will be the judge of what sounds best or most appropriate. So, while the following steps will be applicable for most situations, you shouldn't be afraid to experiment.

Determining the Appropriate Mode for a One-chord Vamp

Let's look at some helpful methods for determining what to play over a one-chord section.

1. **Use the chord's 3rd to choose the major or minor modes.**

   This is pretty self-explanatory. If the chord has a major 3rd (i.e., it's major or a dominant seventh*), you'll start with the three major modes. If it has a minor 3rd (i.e., it's minor, half-diminished†, or diminished), start with the minor modes.

   * Seventh chords will be fully covered in Chapter 10.

   † Half-diminished is another name for a minor seventh flat-five chord, which we'll examine more closely later in the book.

2. **If present, compare the chord's 7th to that of the remaining mode choices.**

   If the chord is a C7, for example, which is spelled C–E–G–B♭, the 7th is B♭. Since the presence of the major 3rd already narrowed down your choice to the three major modes (C Ionian, C Lydian, and C Mixolydian), you can now check those modes to see which has a B♭. Both C Ionian and C Lydian have a B natural, but C Mixolydian has a B♭, which makes it the logical choice.

So let's take a look at a few examples to see how this works. Example 1 is a repetitive groove over a Bm chord, which is spelled B–D–F♯. We know from the minor 3rd (D) that we need a B minor mode. And all three B minor modes (B Dorian, B Phrygian, and B Aeolian) contain the same (minor) 7th (A), so there's nothing more to figure—any of those three choices could technically work.

So let's check out all three options. We're stretching out a bit more here than we might in a typical supportive role—veering somewhat into solo territory—so we can really hear the sound of the modes. Again, if any of the notes shown are in unfamiliar areas of the neck, you can reference Appendix A to find the appropriate scale forms used. Here's what it sounds like using B Dorian:

Example 1

TRACK 59

Now here's what B Aeolian (minor scale) sounds like:

Example 2

TRACK 60

And, finally, here's the B Phrygian approach. Notice the dissonant C major triad arpeggio (the ♭II chord) in measure 8—a unique trait of the Phrygian mode.

Example 3

TRACK 61

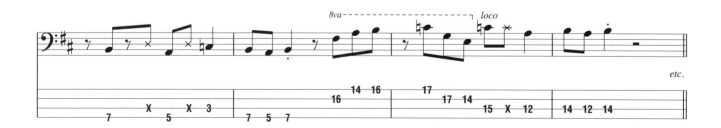

Could you hear the difference? Certain phrases sounded similar, because all three of these modes share several notes—specifically, they share the notes of the B minor pentatonic scale (B–D–E–F♯–A). But occasionally you'd hear the definitive notes—the different 2nds and/or 6ths—that set apart the sound of each. The more you familiarize yourself with the sound of each mode, the quicker you'll be able to determine which one will suit your needs in situations such as these.

If a soloist is going to be playing over an open vamp like this, it's best to decide beforehand (if possible) on the tonality so that everyone will be on the same page. However, once you've thoroughly familiarized yourself with the sound of these modes, you'll be able to hear what the soloist is playing and make the appropriate choice without the aid of spoken cues.

Key Signatures and Modes

If you noticed, the key signature for all three previous examples indicated the key of B minor (two sharps: F♯ and C♯), even though we used B Dorian and B Phrygian in addition to B Aeolian. This helps let the performer know that the tonic here is still B minor, even though we may be playing different modes over the chord. Since these examples were dealing with a brief bit of music, it's not terribly crucial.

But what about a song that uses a mode throughout? There's a bit of debate as to whether *modal key signatures* should be used in these instances or not. In other words, if a song uses the C Lydian mode (which is spelled C–D–E–F♯–G–A–B) throughout its entirety, should you use a C major key signature (no sharps or flats) or a G major key signature (one sharp: F♯)? My vote goes for the C major key signature. Even though the G major key signature would save you from having to write the sharp on the F note over and over, to me, it's more important to show that C is the tonic of the song—not G. However, others feel differently, so there's not a standard approach within the music community.

Example 4 takes place over a G7 vamp. This is a fairly common occurrence if you're playing in a funk band, for instance. Again, we'll look at seventh chords in Chapter 10, but for now, just take my word for it—G7 is spelled G–B–D–F. Since the chord contains a major 3rd, B, we need a major mode: Ionian, Lydian, or Mixolydian. But we also have a seventh tone, F. Since both G Ionian and G Lydian contain an F♯, Mixolydian is the obvious choice.

Example 4

TRACK 62

Remember that these guidelines are not rules. I bring this up now because we've just stated, for all intents and purposes, that the only scale that "works" over a dominant chord is the Mixolydian mode. Of course, anyone who's ever listened to a 12-bar blues knows this is not even close to correct. The minor pentatonic and its close cousin, the blues scale, have been played over dominant chords by soloists for decades with astounding results. It's certainly much less common for us when playing a supportive role, but when we want step out and take the lead, it's a perfectly valid option.

While this practice would theoretically clash—a dominant chord contains a major 3rd, while the minor pentatonic and blues scales contain a minor 3rd—history has shown us that our ears have no problem adapting to this sound when it's used in a certain way. (Interestingly, the opposite approach—using scales with a *major* 3rd over *minor* chords—usually sounds just flat-out wrong to us.) We'll talk about these ideas a bit more later. For now, just remember that these are conventions, not rules.

In Example 4, we were left with only one choice that fit the criteria established by the 3rd and 7th of the chord. But what if the vamp takes place over just a C triad? Just as we tried out all three minor modes over our B minor examples earlier, theoretically, any one of the three major modes would be an option over a C major triad. However, there are a few factors that may aid in the decision:

- **Context:** Does the vamp chord fit within the context of the rest of the song? In other words, does the vamp on a C chord, for example, take place in a song that's in C major, F major, G major, or some other key to which a C chord is diatonic? If so, it will likely sound best to choose the appropriate diatonic mode for the C chord. However, the longer the vamp is, the more liberty you'd have to stretch out a bit into other scales.

- **Melodic or Harmonic Contributions from Other Instruments:** Sometimes the presence of notes played by other instruments may make the decision for you. For example, if you've got a vamp on C, and the guitarist is playing a funk line that includes a B♭, then that would strongly suggest C Mixolydian (C–D–E–F–G–A–B♭). Or maybe the keyboard player is occasionally adding a suspended 4th (F) to the C chord as an ornament. This would make C Lydian an unlikely choice, since it contains an F♯. This type of deduction requires a bit of listening on your part and/or communication with other band members if playing live.

If you're not able to get a sense of the specific tonality when a vamp begins, you might want to avoid certain notes until you're sure. For example, if you're not sure whether the chord is going to be major or minor, you might want to stick with roots and 5ths at first. Once you identify the tonality, you can start bringing the 3rd in. If it's a major chord but you're not sure of the 7th, you could avoid that note by using more major pentatonic lines until the soloist or another instrumentalist tips his/her hand and commits to a major or minor 7th. This type of discretion gets more natural with experience.

WHAT YOU LEARNED:

- How to determine an appropriate mode for playing or soloing over a one-chord vamp by comparing 3rds and 7ths (if applicable).

- How to consider context and contributions from other instruments when making scale choices for playing over a one-chord vamp.

CHAPTER 8: MODAL APPLICATIONS PART 2— NON-DIATONIC CHORDS

Now that you have a firm grip on diatonic harmony and mode construction, it's time to tackle another common harmonic obstacle: that one pesky chord (or several chords) that sounds different than the rest. You know what I'm talking about. The Beatles did this all the time. Think of "Here Comes the Sun," for example. The chord that happens at the end of the second line is a good example, as is the chord that happens during the third chorus line of "All You Need Is Love."

These are called *non-diatonic* chords because they don't normally occur in the key of the song. They contain notes that are outside the tonic major scale and must be given special consideration. In instances like these, the key-center approach will probably work great most of the time, but you're likely to get in trouble over the non-diatonic chord unless you make an adjustment (or stick to nothing but root notes).

By far, the most common non-diatonic chords that you'll encounter will fit into one of two categories: *secondary dominants* or *borrowed chords*. Let's look at each.

SECONDARY DOMINANTS

We've already seen that the V chord in any key is called the dominant chord. This is the chord that wants to resolve up a 4th (or down a 5th) to the tonic (I) chord. Well, a *secondary dominant* is a dominant seventh chord (or sometimes just a major chord) built on a key's scale degree other than the V (in the case of a secondary dominant that's just a major chord, as opposed to a seventh chord, it would be one built on a scale degree other than I, IV, or V).

For example, in the key of C, the ii chord is normally Dm. However, you sometimes see a D7 (or just a D) chord in songs in the key of C, especially in bridge sections. This D or D7 chord is an example of a secondary dominant. In this case, we would say that the D chord is a V/V, which is read "five of five." In other words, it's acting like a temporary dominant chord of the V chord, G. Usually, this chord would be followed by G (V), which would likely be followed by C, the tonic. However, that's not always the case, as we'll discover later on.

In Roman-numeral analysis, you'll see this chord notated as either "V/V," "V7/V" (more common in classical studies), or sometimes "II." The uppercase Roman numeral "II" indicates that a major chord should be played instead of the diatonic minor (ii) chord. Sometimes "II7" will be used to designate that D7 specifically should be played. This is the type of chord (II) referred to in the "Here Comes the Sun" example.

TRACK 63

Another very common secondary dominant is V/IV. In our key of C example, this would mean that our tonic C chord would appear as a C7 instead of just a C triad. In Roman-numeral analysis, you'd either see this as "V/IV" (or "V7/IV") or "I7." This chord would normally be followed by the IV chord (F), as illustrated below.

TRACK 64

Still another one you see often is V/vi. This would mean, in the key of C, that our usually minor iii chord, Em, would be changed to E or E7, as demonstrated here. This is the type of secondary dominant (III) referred to in the "All You Need Is Love" example. It has a very recognizable sound that really pulls the ear to the vi chord.

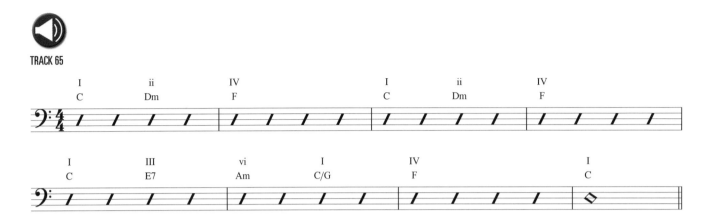

TRACK 65

Scale Choices

OK, so you've heard how these secondary dominant chords sound. But what do you play over them? This can actually be somewhat tricky and requires a bit of forethought. Again, there is more than just one scale that can be used in these instances, but, for now, we're going to look at the most "inside" approach. In the examples that follow, we're playing a few more notes than one might normally play so that we can hear the scales or chord tones against the chords. Obviously, you don't need to play this much. You could play nothing more that root notes (or roots and 5ths) and do just fine in plenty of instances. But when busier bass lines are called for—or if and when you plan to solo—you'll need to have more than roots and 5ths at your disposal.

V of a Major Chord

When the secondary dominant is the V of a *major* chord (V/IV or V/V), use the Mixolydian mode built from the root of the secondary dominant.

Example 1 contains a progression in C that uses a D7 chord, which is a V/V. So, we can use the C major scale for the bulk of it. But, when that D7 chord shows up, we play the D Mixolydian mode. After that, we can switch back to the C major scale.

Example 1

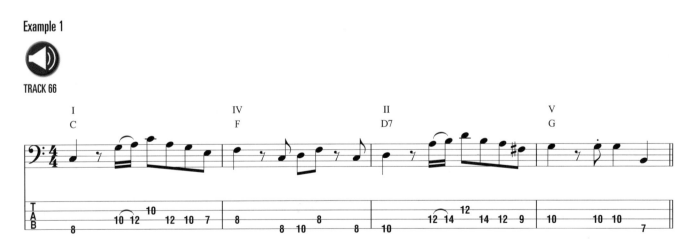

TRACK 66

In Example 2, we see the other possible major-chord-resolving secondary dominant: V/IV. We've changed keys to G major here, so that means our V/IV secondary dominant will be a G7, and we'll play the G Mixolydian mode over that chord. The rest of the lines will come from the G major scale.

Example 2

TRACK 67

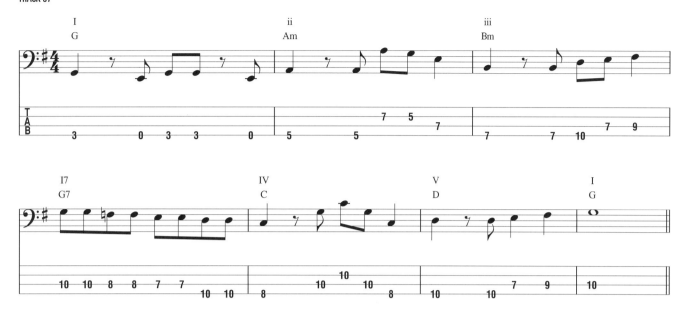

When the secondary dominant is the V of a minor chord, it's a little trickier. The best bet here is to use the harmonic minor scale based on the root of the chord to which the secondary dominant would normally resolve. In other words, if the chord is a V/vi, such as an E7 chord in the key of C, then you'd play an A harmonic minor scale, since Am is the vi chord in C (E7 is the V of Am). There are a few other ways to say this:

1. Play the *harmonic minor scale* that's a 4th above the root of the secondary dominant (A is a 4th above E).

2. Play the *Phrygian dominant scale* based on the root of the secondary dominant. The Phrygian dominant scale is simply a mode of the harmonic minor scale—specifically, the fifth mode. So, if you played the A harmonic minor scale from E to E instead of from A to A, you'd have the E Phrygian dominant mode.

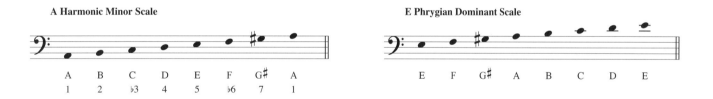

Here's a scale fingering pattern for E Phrygian dominant based around 11th and 12th position:

E Phrygian Dominant

TRACK 68

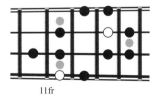

11fr

It's the same set of notes; the only difference lies in which one you consider the root. As long as you use your ear and listen to what you're playing, the name you choose for the scale isn't all that important.

Example 3 demonstrates the sound of the E Phrygian dominant scale (A harmonic minor) against the E7 secondary dominant chord.

Example 3

TRACK 69

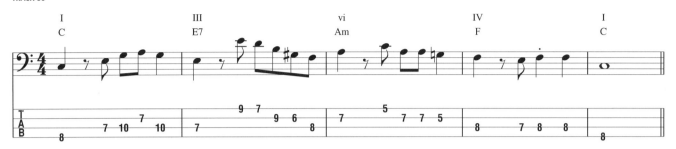

Let's take a look at this same secondary dominant, V/vi, but now in the key A. This would be a C♯ or C♯7 chord, usually resolving to F♯m. Example 4 demonstrates what the C♯ Phrygian dominant scale sounds like over C♯7, with the A major scale covering all the other chords.

Example 4

TRACK 70

Two Ways to Skin a Cat

Remember that you'll sometimes see these secondary dominants with their alternative Roman-numeral analysis, which will be just an uppercase numeral instead of the normal lowercase one. So, in the key of A, for example, you may see a B major chord referred to as "V/V" (V of E, the V chord of A) or simply "II" (as opposed to the normal "ii" used for the diatonic Bm).

Let's take a look at another secondary dominant. Example 5 demonstrates a V/V, or II chord, in the key of D. We've already seen an example of this secondary dominant in Example 1, but this time there's a catch. This II chord is followed by the IV chord instead of the V chord that's expected. This makes the II chord (E) a *non-resolving secondary dominant*. This is just a fancy way of saying it doesn't resolve up a 4th as expected. This particular case—a II chord moving to IV—is particularly common in rock. We still use the same scale (E Mixolydian in this case), but we just need to take care in how we resolve the line.

Example 5

TRACK 71

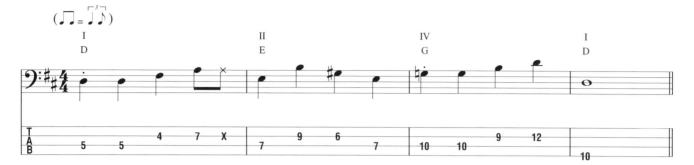

BORROWED CHORDS

The other common non-diatonic chord is the *borrowed* chord. This is a chord that we say is "borrowed" from the parallel mode. Let's say you're in C major, for instance, and you see an Fm chord. Well, Fm normally doesn't appear in C major; it appears in the parallel C minor. So, we call the Fm a borrowed chord. It's more common to borrow from a parallel minor mode while in a major key than it is to borrow from the parallel major mode while in a minor key, so we'll look at examples of the former first.

Major Key Borrowing from Parallel Minor:

The Major ♭VII Chord

Probably the most common borrowed chord of all is the ♭VII. You've heard this chord in about 10,000,000,000 classic rock songs. In the key of C, this would be a B♭ chord.

TRACK 72

The Minor v Chord

Somewhat similar to the ♭VII chord, but not nearly as common, is the minor v chord. In the key of C, this would be a Gm chord.

TRACK 73

The Minor iv Chord

This is one that's heard in lots of Beatles songs. It's a sad, wistful chord that almost always resolves to the tonic I chord. In the key of C, the minor iv would be Fm.

TRACK 74

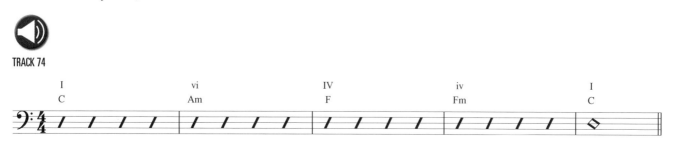

The Major ♭VI Chord

This one has an effect similar to the minor iv chord, but its effect is usually a bit more dramatic than wistful. In the key of C, this would be an A♭ chord.

TRACK 75

The Major ♭III Chord

Classic rock makes good use of this one, as well. If sustained, it can sound dramatic, but it's more often used in passing to add grit to a chordal riff. In the key of C, this would be an E♭ chord.

TRACK 76

Scale Choices

Here's a list of the scales that are commonly played over these borrowed chords.

- **♭VII and v chords:** tonic Mixolydian mode – In the key of C, this would be the C Mixolydian mode over B♭ and Gm chords.

- **iv, ♭VI, and ♭III chords:** tonic Aeolian mode (minor scale) – In the key of C, this would be the C Aeolian mode over Fm, A♭, and E♭ chords.

Again, there are other options, but these are safe and common choices. Let's hear what they sound like. We'll stay in the key of C so that you can hear all the different sounds against a common tonic, but you should work on transposing these ideas to all the keys.

Example 6 features the C Mixolydian mode over the ♭VII chord, B♭. The C major scale and/or C major pentatonic scales handle the rest of the chords.

Example 6

TRACK 77

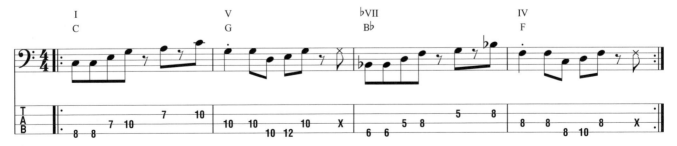

Example 7 makes use of the minor v chord, Gm, over which we play C Mixolydian. The rest is C major. Notice how similar the Mixolydian lick is to Example 6.

Example 7

We get treated to the minor iv chord in Example 8. In the key of C, this is an Fm chord. We're playing the C major scale until then, at which point we switch to the C minor scale.

Example 8

Check out the dramatic sound of the ♭VI chord, A♭, in Example 9. We're playing the C major scale over all the chords except for that one, switching at that point to the parallel C minor scale.

Example 9

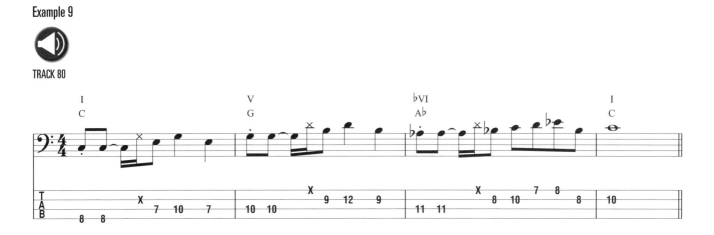

Example 10 demonstrates the classic-rock-tinged ♭III chord with a ballsy riff that makes typical use of the chord (i.e., as a connector between I and IV). In the key of C, the ♭III is an E♭ chord. We play C major pentatonic over the I chord, use E♭ major pentatonic over the E♭ chord (which is the relative major of C minor pentatonic—same notes, different name), and F major pentatonic over F.

Example 10

TRACK 81

Minor Key Borrowing from Parallel Major:

The Major V Chord

As we mentioned earlier, it's very common to substitute a major V chord for a minor v chord, and this is essentially borrowing this harmony from the parallel major. In the key of C minor, this would be a G chord.

TRACK 82

The Major IV Chord

This is another very common one that you'll hear in lots of classic rock and R&B. In the key of C minor, this would be an F chord.

TRACK 83

The Minor ii Chord

This one has a bit of a jazzy sound to it. Think of Van Morrison's "Moondance" for an example of this. In the key of C minor, this would be a D minor chord.

TRACK 84

Scale Choices

Here's a list of the scales that are commonly played over these borrowed chords.

- **Major V chord:** tonic harmonic minor scale – In the key of C minor, this would be the C harmonic minor scale over a G chord.
- **Major IV and minor ii chords:** tonic Dorian mode – In the key of C minor, this would be the C Dorian mode over F and Dm chords.

Again, there are other scales to experiment with; these are just the common choices. Let's hear what they sound like.

In Example 11, we hear the sound of the major V chord, G. After using the C minor scale in measures 1–3, we switch to C harmonic minor over the G chord to acknowledge the change of B♭ to B.

Example 11

TRACK 85

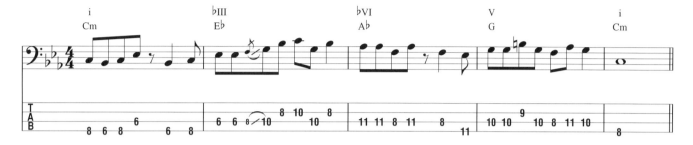

Example 12 lets us hear how the C Dorian mode sounds over a major IV chord, F. We stick to C minor pentatonic the rest of the time.

Example 12

TRACK 86

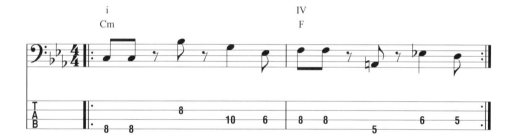

Finally, we hear the jazzy minor ii chord, Dm, in Example 13 and play over it with C Dorian; otherwise, it's straight C minor.

Example 13

TRACK 87

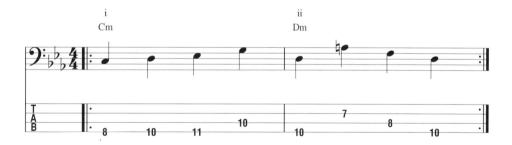

WHAT YOU LEARNED:

- Two common non-diatonic chords: **secondary dominants** and **borrowed chords**.
- Typical scale choices for common secondary dominants and borrowed chords.

CHAPTER 9: MODAL APPLICATIONS PART 3— MODAL PROGRESSIONS

Now that you're familiar with modes and the concept of borrowed chords, it's time to introduce *modal progressions*. A modal progression is one that's built upon chords from a harmonized mode. Just as we've already harmonized two modes—Ionian and Aeolian (also known as the major and minor scales, respectively)—we can harmonize other modes to form triads from them. When we play over a modal progression, we simply use the mode from which the chords are derived.

For example, if a song is in C Mixolydian, we'd use the C Mixolydian mode. If it's in E Dorian, we'd use the E Dorian mode. It's just like the key-center approach we used earlier, only we're using modes other than just Ionian (major scale) and Aeolian (minor scale).

MIXOLYDIAN MODE

The Mixolydian mode is commonly used for progressions. When we harmonize each note of a Mixolydian mode, using the same stacking 3rds method as in Chapter 2, we get yet another set of seven triads. Here they are in the key of C:

TRACK 88

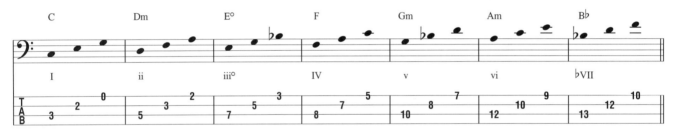

When a song is in a Mixolydian mode (or sometimes you hear "Mixolydian key"), it uses these chords as the foundation—not the set of triads from the major scale. Generally speaking, if you have a song that clearly identifies a C chord as the tonic, yet you repeatedly see a B♭ chord (♭VII) and no G major or G7 chord, it's a safe bet that the song is using the Mixolydian mode. Let's look at a few examples, again in the key of C.

Example 1 makes use of a time-tested classic rock progression: I–♭VII–IV. These three chords may have been in as many songs as I–VI–V (in the '70s at least!).

Example 1

TRACK 89

Example 2 is a mellower example that uses some other chords from the C Mixolydian mode, including the minor v chord, Gm.

Example 2

🔊

TRACK 90

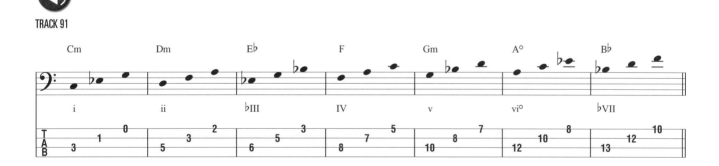

DORIAN MODE

The other mode commonly used to build progressions is the Dorian mode. A tell-tale sign of a Dorian progression is often a minor tonic (i) with a major IV chord. The characteristic trait of the Dorian mode is the natural 6th degree (as opposed to the ♭6th of Aeolian), and that's exactly what the major IV chord highlights; its major 3rd is the natural 6th of the scale. This is a very common sound in rock, blues-rock, jazz, and pop. When we harmonize the C Dorian mode, we get the following set of triads:

🔊

TRACK 91

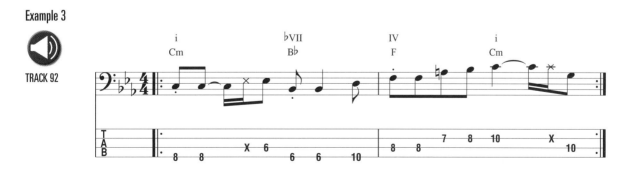

In Example 3, we rock out with the C Dorian mode over a Tom Petty-style progression. The major IV chord is prominently displayed here.

Example 3

🔊

TRACK 92

Example 4 is a much more moody-sounding progression in C Dorian and highlights another common Dorian device: the minor ii chord. Normally, the triad built on the second degree in a minor scale would be diminished. The presence of Dm here results in the Dorian tonality. We're deliberately playing arpeggios here in a walking style so you can hear the scale at work; a much more minimal note choice strategy would work fine, as well.

Example 4

TRACK 93

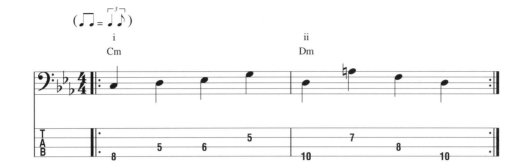

Notice, again, that the key signature used here indicates C minor (three flats). Even though we're adding a natural sign to every A that's played, the three flats in the key signature make it clear to the performer that C is the tonic.

Besides Ionian and Aeolian, those are really the only two modes that are consistently used. You will occasionally see a song in a Lydian mode (guitarists such as Joe Satriani and Steve Vai are good examples, as is the theme song from *the Simpsons*), but it's a rarity by comparison.

How Do You Tell Borrowed Chords from a Modal Progression?

This is a good question, and the line can certainly be blurred between the two. Generally, if the song is using chords exclusively from the mode (Dorian or Mixolydian, for example), then you'd call it a modal progression. If a song uses chords from the major or minor scale that contradict the modal chords, then you'd probably label the chords that don't fit as borrowed chords.

For example, let's say you're in the key of C, and you have the following progression:

TRACK 94

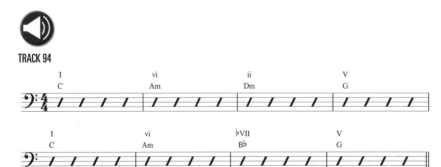

The only chord non-diatonic to C major is the B♭ chord. However, we also have a V chord (G) in the progression, which contains the note B. We can't call this a modal progression, because not all the chords belong to one mode. Therefore, the song is in C major, and the B♭ (♭VII) would be called a borrowed chord.

Let's close out the chapter with a few examples that are more "soloistic."

Example 5 takes place over a B Dorian progression and makes use of some imitative rhythmic phrasing.

Example 5

TRACK 95

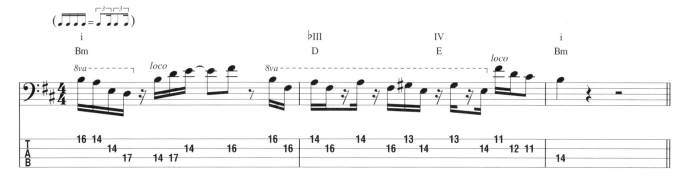

In Example 6, we're playing F Mixolydian over a I–IV–v–I progression. Note how the chord tones are carefully targeted throughout.

Example 6

TRACK 96

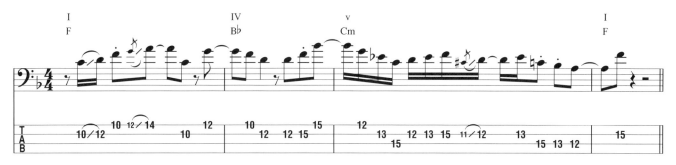

WHAT YOU LEARNED:

- How to harmonize the Mixolydian and Dorian modes.
- How to determine if a song is using a modal progression.
- Mixolydian and Dorian are the most commonly used modal progressions (aside from Ionian and Aeolian).
- Tell-tale signs of a Mixolydian progression are a major I chord with a major ♭VII chord or minor v chord.
- Tell-tale signs of a Dorian progression are a minor i chord with a major IV chord or a minor ii chord.

CHAPTER 10: SEVENTH CHORDS AND EXTENDED HARMONY

Triads make up a large portion of the chords we encounter, but there are others that frequently crop up, as well. In this chapter, we'll take a look at *seventh chords* and *extended harmony*. We've briefly touched upon seventh chords in previous chapters, but now we'll examine them more closely.

SEVENTH CHORDS

Whereas triads contain three different notes, seventh chords contain four different notes. Now that you understand how triads are built, sevenths should seem like a logical next step. We build them by stacking yet another 3rd on top of the triad.

If we stack another diatonic 3rd on top of our diatonic triads in the key of C, for example, we'll end up with several different types of seventh chords:

TRACK 97

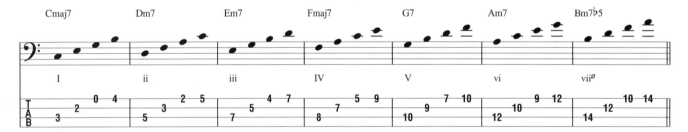

Notice that the Roman numerals haven't changed, because all the chord functions are still the same. They're just a little dressier as seventh chords. We see four different types of seventh chords within the diatonic scale:

1. **Major seventh** (maj7)

2. **Minor seventh** (m7)

3. **Dominant seventh** (7)

4. **Minor seven flat-five** (m7♭5)

Again, this is the diatonic seventh chord formula for any major key:

maj7 (I), m7 (ii), m7 (iii), maj7 (IV), 7 (V), m7 (vi), and m7♭5 (vii⌀)*

*The circle with a line through it (⌀) is the symbol for half-diminished, which is another name for minor seventh flat-five.

Let's look at each type of seventh chord, with C as the root so we can see the formula for each one. First is a major seventh (maj7), which is spelled 1–3–5–7. This is a major triad with a major 3rd stacked on top, or a major triad with a major 7th interval (from the root) added. Here's Cmaj7:

TRACK 98

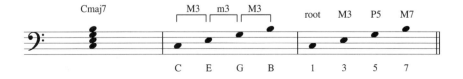

Next let's look at the dominant seventh (7), which is spelled 1–3–5–♭7. It's the same as a major seventh, but the top note (the 7th) has been lowered to a minor 7th interval. Here's C7:

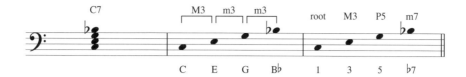

Now here's the minor seventh (m7), which is spelled 1–♭3–5–♭7. Compared to the major seventh, it has a lowered 3rd and a lowered 7th. Here's Cm7:

And now here's the minor seventh flat-five (m7♭5), or half-diminished, chord. Compared to the major seventh, it has a lowered 3rd, lowered 5th, and lowered 7th. Here's Cm7♭5:

These tones (7ths) are another possibility to consider when creating a bass line or soloing. Depending on the chord, major sevenths in particular, you may not want to completely resolve your lines on them, but they're nice to highlight occasionally for a bit more color. Let's take a look at some common seventh chord arpeggio shapes (you can find more in the Appendix A).

Major Seventh (1–3–5–7)

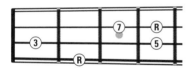
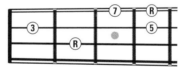

Dominant Seventh (1–3–5–♭7)

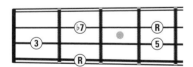
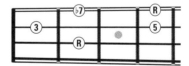

Minor Seventh (1–♭3–5–♭7)

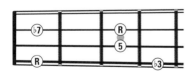
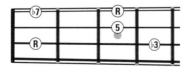

Minor Seventh Flat-Five (1–♭3–♭5–♭7)

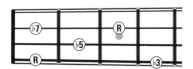
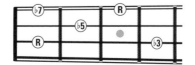

And now let's check out some examples that highlight the seventh tones. In Example 1, we have a I–IV progression in C major: C–F. For each chord, we're playing major seventh arpeggios, which illustrate a good point: just because you're playing over a triad doesn't mean you can't include the 7th.

Example 1

TRACK 102

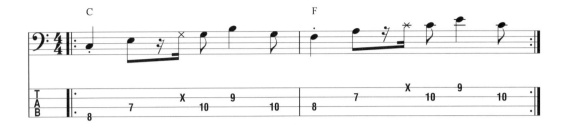

Example 2 takes place over a G7 chord and highlights the ♭7th (F) significantly.

Example 2

TRACK 103

How Do You Tell Borrowed Chords from a Modal Progression?

Pretty much everything we've covered in regard to non-diatonic triads applies to seventh chords, too. This means that, instead of a IV chord being a major seventh, it could appear as a dominant seventh, for example. It also means that we could see our non-diatonic triads turned into seventh chords. For example, in the key of C, a major II chord (V/V) could be a D7 instead of just a D. Or a borrowed B♭ chord (♭VII) could appear as a B♭maj7 or even a B♭7.

Each one of these examples presents its own challenge. Sometimes, the facts that they're seventh chords won't require any additional adjustment. In other words, the same scale (D Mixolydian) you use for a D chord (II) in the key of C would work equally well over a D7. This is because the 7th of D7 is C, and therefore it doesn't add any additional conflicts to the scale.

A B♭maj7 chord (♭VII) in the key of C could also be handled by the same scale used to handle a B♭ triad: C Mixolydian. Again, this is because the 7th of B♭maj7 (A) is contained within that C Mixolydian mode. A B♭7 chord in the key of C, however, would be a different story. It's still a ♭VII chord, but the 7th of B♭7 is A♭, and A♭ is not contained within C Mixolydian. For this type of chord, you'd need another type of scale, which could be a B♭ Mixolydian or possibly B♭ Lydian dominant. The Lydian dominant scale is a mode of the melodic minor scale, which is beyond the scope of this book, but you can think of Lydian dominant as a Mixolydian scale with a ♯4th degree. Its numeric formula is 1–2–3–♯4–5–6–♭7.

Let's take a look at a few more examples using non-diatonic seventh chords that can still be covered with the scales and modes we've learned this far. Example 3 is built from a I–V–IV–♭VII progression in G, using an Fmaj7 as the ♭VII chord. As with the ♭VII triad, the tonic Mixolydian mode (G Mixolydian) will still cover this chord nicely since the 7th of Fmaj7 (E) is contained within that mode.

Example 3

TRACK 104

Example 4 is a funky example using a tonic dominant seventh chord (B7) and a dominant seventh IV chord (E7). For this, we'll switch between each chord's respective Mixolydian mode: B Mixolydian over B7 and E Mixolydian over E7.

Example 4

TRACK 105

Example 5 will require you to put your thinking cap on. We're in D minor here. Along with a tonic minor seventh (Dm7), we move through a dominant IV chord (G7) and a dominant V chord (A7). This requires three different scales. D minor (or D minor pentatonic) will handle the Dm7 chords, but we'll use G Mixolydian over the G7 and D harmonic minor (a.k.a. A Phrygian dominant) over the A7.

Example 5

TRACK 106

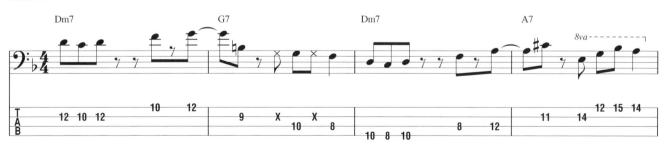

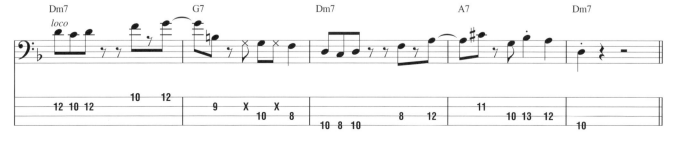

EXTENSIONS

Beyond seventh chords, we can still continue the process of stacking 3rds to get what we call *extensions*, or *extended harmony*. In a seventh chord, we stacked 3rds three times: root, 3rd, 5th, and 7th. With extended chords, we continue to stack yet more 3rds on top of that.

Stacking one more 3rd on top of a 7th gives us what we call the 9th. It's the same note as the 2nd, only an octave higher, so we call it a 9th. For example, here's our Cmaj7 chord again:

The 7th of the chord is B. What's a 3rd above B? It's D. So when we stack a D on top, we get a Cmaj9 chord.

TRACK 107

Why do we call it a 9th instead of a 2nd? The basic rule is this: If the chord contains a 7th, then you call this note a 9th. If it doesn't contain a 7th, you'd call this note a 2nd. The chord above is a ninth chord because the 7th (B) is present. Specifically, it's a Cmaj9 chord because it contains a major 3rd (E) and a major 7th. Just as with seventh chords, we can alter notes to get different types of ninth chords:

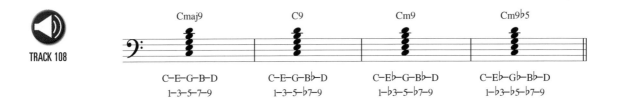
TRACK 108

It's beyond the scope of this book to fully cover extensions because it's an expansive topic and quite a big can of worms (you can continue stacking more 3rds to get 11th chords and even 13th chords). Extensions such as the 9th, 11th, and 13th of a chord tend to sound better when played in the higher registers, where they tend not to muddy things up by rubbing too closely to the root, 3rd, 5th, etc.

Also realize that you don't necessarily have to be playing over a ninth chord for you to highlight the 9th in your phrases (by the same token, you don't need to be playing over seventh chords to highlight the 7ths). You could superimpose a major 9th sound over even just a major triad by including the 7th and 9th in your line. It's helpful to learn the chords because it'll help get the sound of the harmonies in your ear. But, when creating lines or soloing, the use of all of these notes is at your discretion.

Example 6 demonstrates this idea with a solo line over a progression in C. Over the tonic I chord, we're playing the B and D notes at the peak of our run, creating a Cmaj9 "sound" over the C triad.

Example 6

WHAT YOU LEARNED:

- By stacking another 3rd on top of a triad, we create **seventh chords**.

- There are four types of diatonic seventh chords: **major seventh** (maj7), **minor seventh** (m7), **dominant seventh** (7), and **minor seventh flat-five** (m7♭5).

- Non-diatonic chords can appear as seventh chords and may require an alternate scale choice, depending on whether the 7th is contained within the mode.

- We can continue to stack 3rds on top of seventh chords to create ninth, 11th, and 13th chords.

- These 7ths and extensions (9ths, 11ths, and 13ths) can be accented as color tones when playing solos, and extensions that are sustained for any period of time normally sound better in higher registers.

CHAPTER 11: THE NOTES IN-BETWEEN THE NOTES

Aside from the pentatonic scales, all the scales we looked at in this book contain seven notes. However, there are 12 notes in all. What about the other five? Do we simply have to avoid them? Absolutely not! They can all be used effectively with a bit of finesse. In this chapter, we're going to look at some common ways to implement some of these "in-between" notes in colorful ways.

PASSING TONES

Probably the most common use for non-diatonic notes in bass lines is as *passing tones*. This name is fairly self-explanatory and refers to tones that are used to pass between two other tones. Passing tones can be diatonic, too. If you move from the root of a C chord (C) to D and then up to the chord's 3rd (E), the D note is acting as a passing tone. We've seen examples of this idea throughout the book, although they weren't labeled as such. However, passing tones can also be non-diatonic, and that's the kind we'll look at here.

The ♭3rd (a.k.a. ♯2nd) over a Major Chord

This is a classic spot where you'll find a chromatic passing tone. If we're playing over a C chord, for example, this would mean playing D–D♯–E. (Depending on the musical context, you may find this passing tone named E♭, as well.) Let's have a listen to this type of idea in a I–IV progression in C. This should sound familiar.

Example 1

TRACK 110

Here's an example of this device in a funky line that moves from G to C7. Note that we're using the same passing-note motive relative to each chord—A–A♯–B over the G chord and D–D♯–E over the C7 chord. As you may have recognized, the C7 chord here is non-diatonic (a Cmaj7 chord would be diatonic to G major), and we acknowledge this by using the C Mixolydian mode (save for the chromatic D♯ passing tone) for this chord, characterized by the B♭ at the end of measure 2.

Example 2

TRACK 111

The ♭5th (a.k.a. ♯4th) over a Minor Chord

Although this move occurs more often over a minor chord, it can appear over a major chord, as well—especially when working out of the Mixolydian mode. But we'll look at minor applications here. In fact, it's so common in minor applications that there's a scale that includes this passing tone: the blues scale. It's just like the minor pentatonic scale, but it has the added ♭5th tone. Here's a fingering for the A blues scale in fifth position:

A Blues Scale

TRACK 112

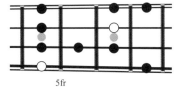

And here's how we might use this tone in a line for an A Dorian progression of Am–D.

Example 3

TRACK 113

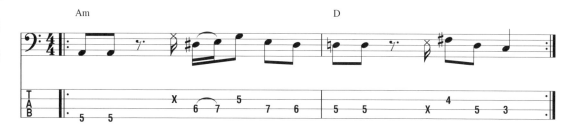

Let's use the same idea and progression again, but this time we'll solo in the upper register.

Example 4

TRACK 114

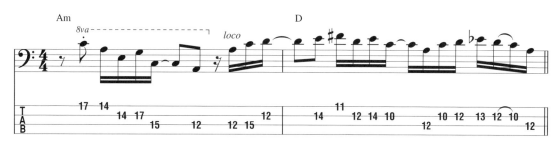

The Major 7th over a Minor or Dominant Chord

This is another common move in funky styles. In C, this would mean using B as a passing tone over a Cm, Cm7, or C7 chord. Let's check it out over a C7 groove first.

Example 5

TRACK 115

And now let's hear it in a line that takes place over a i–♭VI progression in Cm: Cm–A♭. We use the B passing tone in descending fashion over the i chord and then in ascending fashion over the ♭VI chord to climb back up to the tonic.

Example 6

You'll find that, with practice, just about any note can be used as a passing tone. Some may sound better up in a soloing register, but they can certainly work. Experiment with altering the previous examples to incorporate other passing tones and see what you can come up with.

OTHER USES

Aside from passing tones, these notes can be used in other colorful ways, as well; they don't have to appear between two diatonic tones. Let's check out a few examples of this. Here's a funky line in D that moves from D7 to G7. Over the D7, we make use of the ♭3rd (F) in a motive that climbs to the root of the G chord via F and F♯. Note how this idea is imitated (though not directly transposed) in measure 4, where we climb up to D via B and C.

Example 7

In this example in E, we see a nifty device called *enclosure*. This involves "enclosing" a target note with the chromatic notes surrounding it. In our case, we have a I–III–vi–IV progression, and we're enclosing the roots of the III chord (G♯) and vi chord (C♯m), first playing the note a half step above, then the note a half step below, and finally the root. This goes by pretty quickly, so the effect isn't terribly disconcerting; it comes off more as a nice ornament.

Example 8

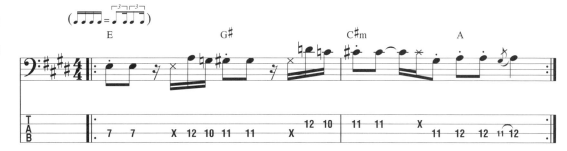

Another option is the *approach tone*. This simply involves approaching a root note via a half step above or below. This is a very common device in jazz and blues. Here's a stripped-down example in the key of A that uses a I–vi–ii–V progression: A–F#m–Bm–E7. Note that each chord's root is preceded by a note that lies one half step above or below it.

Example 9

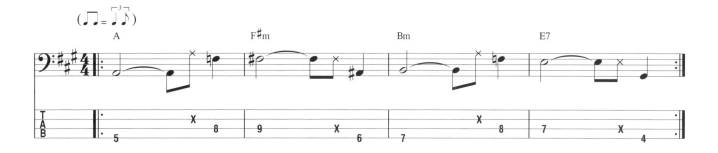

The sky's really the limit when it comes to using these chromatic notes. Experience will be your best teacher in determining when and why they will work, but the concepts presented here are certainly a good start.

WHAT YOU LEARNED:

- **Passing tones** are notes used to pass from one chord tone or scale tone to another. They can be diatonic or chromatic.

- Commonly used passing tones include the ♭**3rd** (over major or dominant chords), ♭**5th** (over minor or dominant chords), and **major 7th** (over minor or dominant chords).

- Other uses for non-diatonic tones include **enclosure** (surrounding a chord tone with notes a half step above and below it or vice versa) and **approach tones** (preceding a root note by a note a half step above or below).

- Any non-diatonic tone should be used with care. Unless you're soloing, it's best to resolve to the root or another chord tone on the strong beats.

CONCLUSION

Well, that's a wrap! We've covered a bunch of ground, so be sure to re-read the sections that are still foggy. It's a lot of information to take in, and it will probably be a while before you're able to assimilate everything and apply it on a regular basis. Familiarity with these concepts comes with practice and experience. Keep your ears open and actively *listen* to what you play. Many times, this act alone makes the difference between something musical and something mechanical.

There's still much more to learn, which is what makes the study of music such a rewarding journey. Here are some recommendations for further study:

- **Learn Melodies:** This can't be stressed enough. Lots of people don't realize it, but the simple act of learning a melody can do wonders for your musicianship. It helps you make important scale/chord connections automatically, helps you keep your place within the form, and gives you ideas with which to play around. Even if you don't ever plan on soloing much, playing melodies can't help but develop your harmonic awareness, which can only strengthen your musical instincts all around.

- **Sing!** Lots of people say they can't sing. Some people certainly have more of a gift for it than others. But, for a musician, there's simply no better way to train your ear than to practice singing what you play and vice versa. You'll learn to link your ear with your hands much quicker, in my opinion, and who knows … you may end up enjoying it! Another added benefit is that it will make you more marketable as a player (bands are always looking for good backup vocalists).

- **Listen to Other Instruments:** This is a great way to gather new ideas. The phrases that a pianist plays, for instance, are idiomatic to that instrument. Arranging licks from another instrument for the bass can be an eye-opening (and ear-opening) experience.

- **Set Short-term Goals:** Setting goals keeps you focused on improving and trying new things, as opposed to falling into the same old, predictable patterns.

- **Play with Other Musicians:** Interaction with other players is incredibly inspiring in many ways. And you'll pick up things from others simply because they have a different way of looking at music than you do. Again, this doesn't just include bassists; any and every instrument has something to offer in this regard.

Be sure to check out the appendixes that follow. All of the scales that we looked at are shown in several different shapes, each covering the entire neck. There are also play-along tracks of common progressions with which you can practice your newfound skills. Good luck!

APPENDIX A: SCALE REFERENCE

This appendix contains all the scales covered in this book, presented with C as the root. Be sure to practice these in all keys.

> NOTE: The "Shape" numbers system that I've used with these scales is not a standard in the bass community; many people have their own way of organizing and cataloging scale shapes on the neck. This is just the method that makes sense to me: Shape 1 is the one in which the tonic of the scale appears as the first note on string 4. No open strings are used in these shapes, so they're all completely moveable. Once the notes reach above fret 12, the shape is brought down to the lower octave. The tonic (C) is shown as an open (white) circle in each diagram.

C MAJOR SCALE (IONIAN)

Shape 1

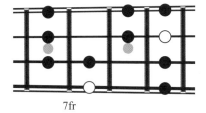

7fr

Shape 2

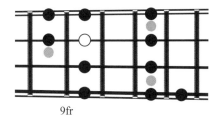

9fr

Shape 3

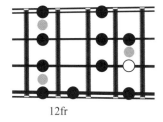

12fr

Shape 4

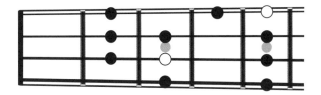

Shape 5

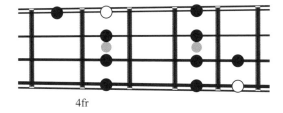

4fr

C MAJOR PENTATONIC SCALE

Shape 1

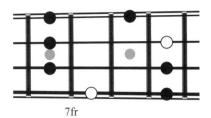

7fr

Shape 2

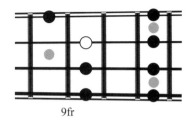

9fr

Shape 3

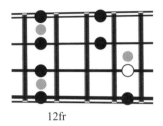

12fr

Shape 4

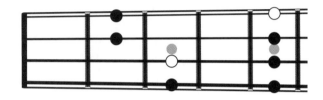

Shape 5

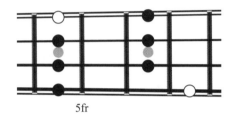

5fr

C MINOR SCALE (AEOLIAN)

Shape 1

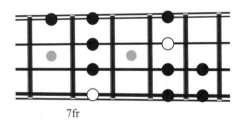

7fr

Shape 2

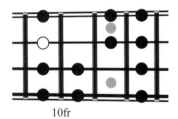

10fr

Shape 3

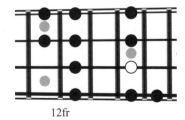

12fr

Shape 4

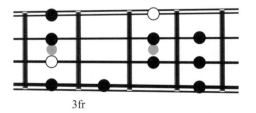

3fr

Shape 5

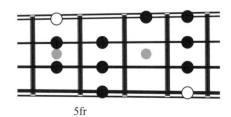

5fr

C MINOR PENTATONIC SCALE

Shape 1

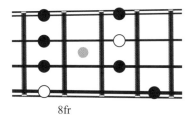

8fr

Shape 2

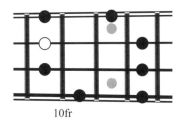

10fr

Shape 3

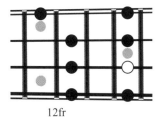

12fr

Shape 4

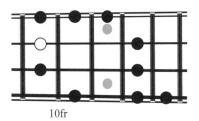

3fr

Shape 5

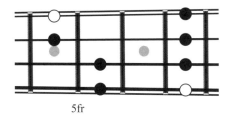

5fr

C BLUES SCALE

Shape 1

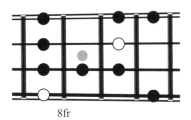

8fr

Shape 2

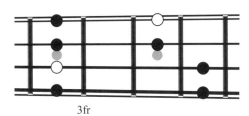

10fr

Shape 3

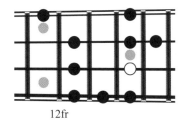

12fr

Shape 4

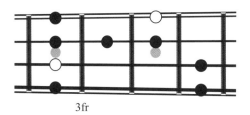

3fr

Shape 5

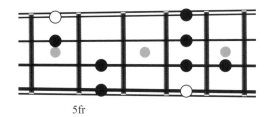

5fr

C DORIAN

Shape 1

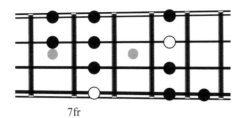

7fr

Shape 2

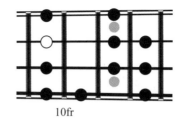

10fr

Shape 3

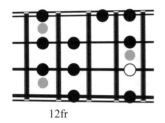

12fr

Shape 4

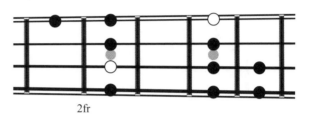

2fr

Shape 5

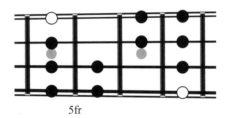

5fr

C PHRYGIAN

Shape 1

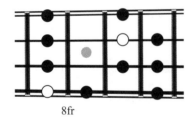

8fr

Shape 2

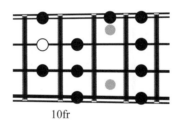

10fr

Shape 3

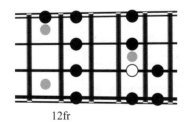

12fr

Shape 4

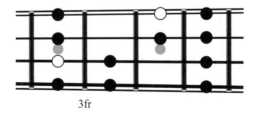

3fr

Shape 5

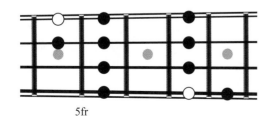

5fr

C LYDIAN

Shape 1

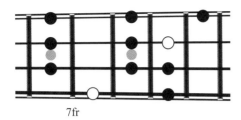

7fr

Shape 2

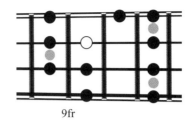

9fr

Shape 3

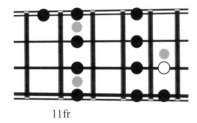

11fr

Shape 4

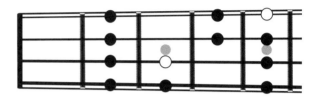

Shape 5

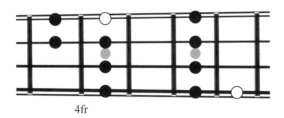

4fr

C MIXOLYDIAN

Shape 1

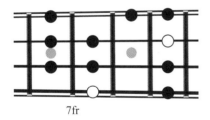

7fr

Shape 2

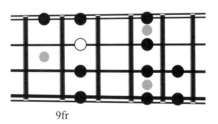

9fr

Shape 3

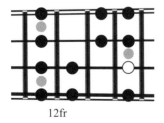

12fr

Shape 4

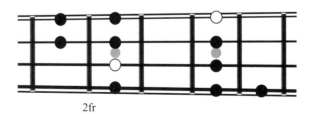

2fr

Shape 5

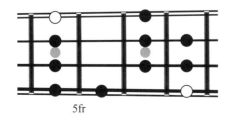

5fr

C LOCRIAN

Shape 1

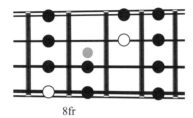

8fr

Shape 2

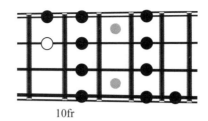

10fr

Shape 3

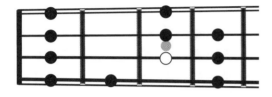

Shape 4

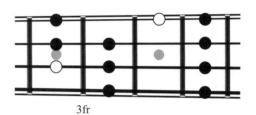

3fr

Shape 5

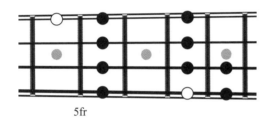

5fr

C HARMONIC MINOR

Shape 1

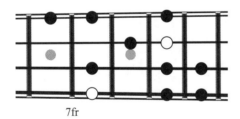

7fr

Shape 2

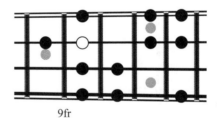

9fr

Shape 3

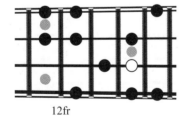

12fr

Shape 4

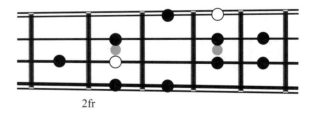

2fr

Shape 5

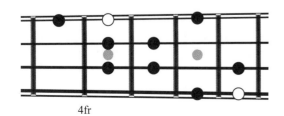

4fr

C MAJOR ARPEGGIOS

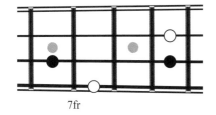

7fr

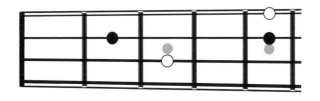

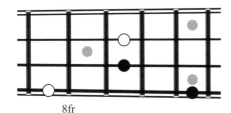

8fr

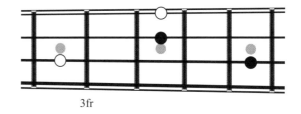

3fr

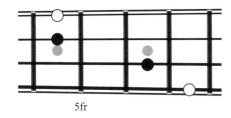

5fr

C MINOR ARPEGGIOS

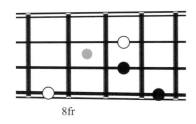

8fr

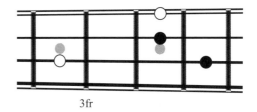

3fr

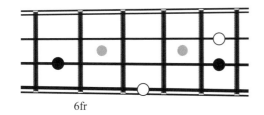

6fr

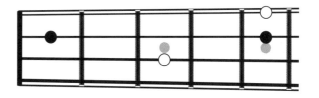

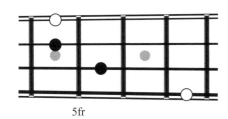

5fr

C DIMINISHED ARPEGGIOS

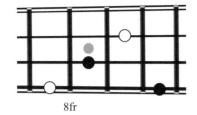

8fr

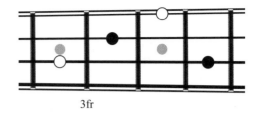

3fr

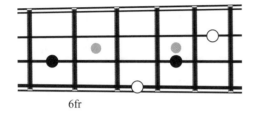

6fr

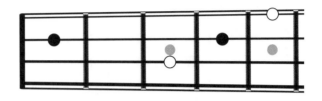

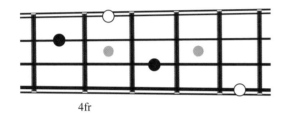

4fr

C AUGMENTED ARPEGGIOS

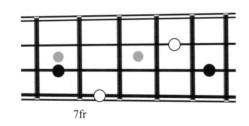

7fr

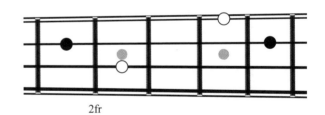

2fr

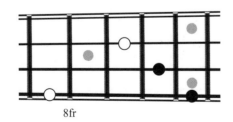

8fr

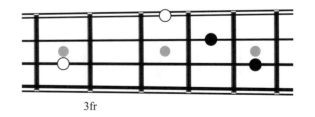

3fr

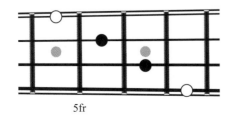

5fr

C MAJOR SEVENTH ARPEGGIOS

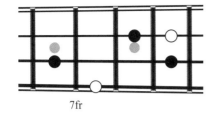

7fr

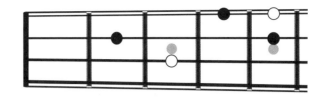

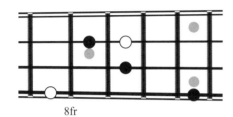

8fr

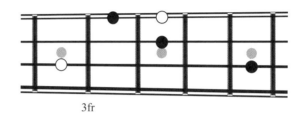

3fr

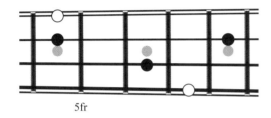

5fr

C DOMINANT SEVENTH ARPEGGIOS

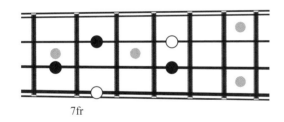

7fr

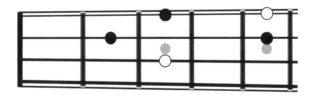

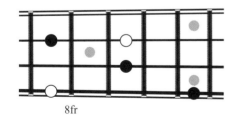

8fr

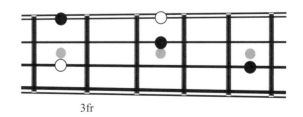

3fr

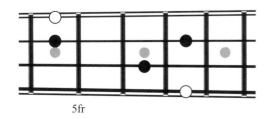

5fr

C MINOR SEVENTH ARPEGGIOS

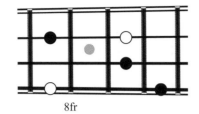

8fr

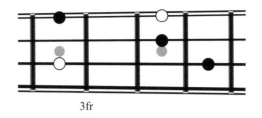

3fr

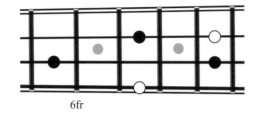

6fr

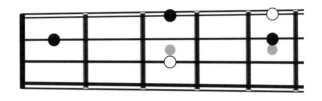

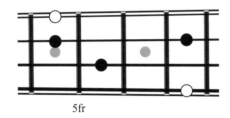

5fr

C MINOR SEVENTH FLAT-FIVE ARPEGGIOS

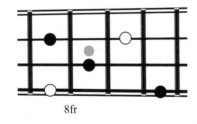

8fr

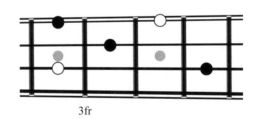

3fr

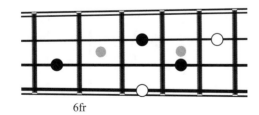

6fr

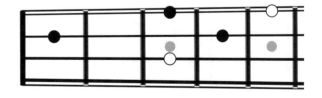

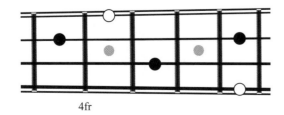

4fr

C DIMINISHED SEVENTH ARPEGGIOS

This is also known as a *fully diminished seventh* chord. It's a symmetrical chord consisting of nothing but stacked minor 3rd intervals. It can be found on the seventh degree of a harmonized harmonic minor scale.

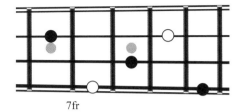

7fr

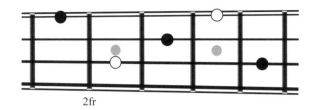

2fr

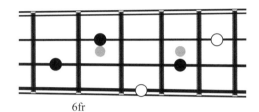

6fr

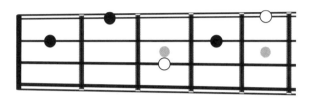

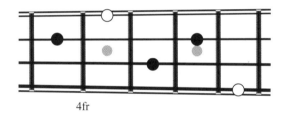

4fr

FULL NECK DIAGRAM

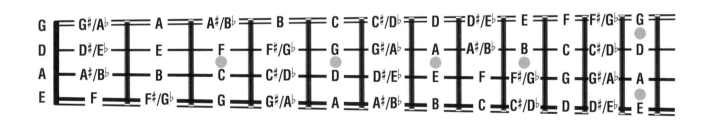

APPENDIX B: CHORD PROGRESSIONS AND PLAY-ALONG TRACKS

Here are several common progressions with "minus-bass" tracks for you to practice over. I've included suggested scales to use when generating bass lines for or soloing over most of them.

MAJOR AND MINOR DIATONIC PROGRESSIONS

Progression #1: I–IV in C major
Scale suggestion: C major scale

Progression #2: I–IV–V–I in E major
Scale suggestion: E major scale

Progression #3: I–V–vi–IV in D major
Scale suggestion: D major scale

Progression #4: i–♭VI–♭VII–i in C minor
Scale suggestion: C minor scale

Progression #5: i–♭III–♭VI–iv in F♯ minor
Scale suggestion: F♯ minor scale

MAJOR AND MINOR PROGRESSIONS WITH NON-DIATONIC CHORDS

Progression #6: I–I7–IV–iv in G major
Scale suggestions: I and IV: G major scale; I7: G Mixolydian; iv: G minor scale

Progression #7: I–♭VI–♭VII–IV in B major
Scale suggestions: I and IV: B major scale; ♭VI and ♭VII: B minor scale

TRACK 126

Progression #8: i–♭VII–IV–V in A minor
Scale suggestions: I and ♭VII: A minor scale; IV: A Dorian (same notes as D Mixolydian);
V: A harmonic minor (same notes as E Phrygian dominant)

TRACK 127

Progression #9: i–♭III–IV–♭VI in E minor
Scale suggestions: i, ♭III, and ♭VI: E minor scale; IV: E Dorian (same notes as A Mixolydian)

TRACK 128

MODAL PROGRESSIONS

Progression #10: I–♭VII–IV in E major
Scale suggestion: E Mixolydian

TRACK 129

Progression #11: I–IV–v–IV in F major
Scale suggestion: F Mixolydian

TRACK 130

Progression #12: i–♭VII–IV–i in B minor
Scale suggestion: B Dorian

TRACK 131

Progression #13: i–IV7 in D minor
Scale suggestion: D Dorian

TRACK 132

BLUES PROGRESSIONS

Progression #14: 12-bar shuffle blues in A major
Scale suggestions: I: A Mixolydian; IV: D Mixolydian; V: E Mixolydian;
the A blues scale will also work over the whole form when soloing.

TRACK 133

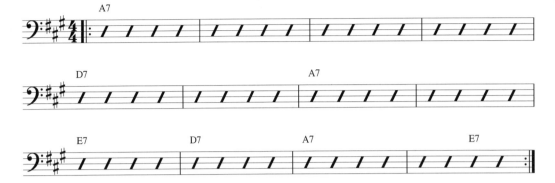

Progression #15: 12-bar funk blues in C major
Scale suggestions: I: C Mixolydian; IV: F Mixolydian; V: G Mixolydian;
the C blues scale will also work over the whole form when soloing.

TRACK 134

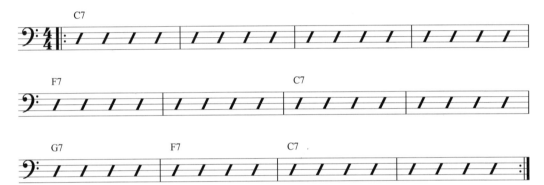

Progression #16: 12-bar rock blues in B minor
Scale suggestions: i: B minor pentatonic or B Dorian; iv: E Dorian; ♭VI: G Lydian (same notes as B Aeolian);
V: F♯ Phrygian dominant; the B blues scale will also work over the whole form when soloing.

TRACK 135

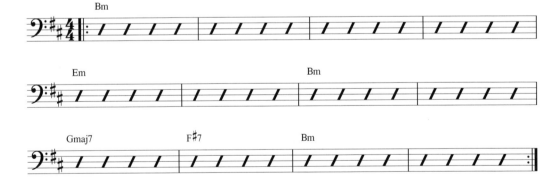

Progression #17: 8-bar slow shuffle blues in D major
Scale suggestions: I: D Mixolydian; IV: G Mixolydian; V: A Mixolydian;
the D blues scale will also work over the whole form when soloing.

TRACK 136

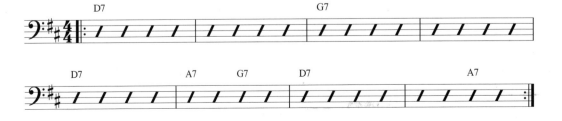